# Contents

D0265943

# Introduction

## About this book

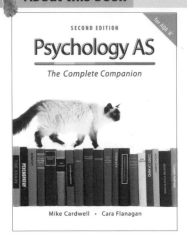

SECOND EDITION

**Psychology AS**

*The Complete Companion*

for AQA 'A'

Mike Cardwell · Cara Flanagan

This book is a mini version of *Psychology AS: The Complete Companion*. It contains just the basic information needed for the AQA specification A AS examination. There are no frills and no extras.

When a cook makes a special sauce he or she will boil the liquid for a long time so that it reduces in volume leaving just the most essential (and tasty) ingredients. That's what we have done here – produced the nuggets of knowledge necessary to enable you to focus on what you *must* learn in order to do well in the exam, as distinct from what you *could* learn. In order to make the most of the material presented in this book you should use it alongside the *AS Complete Companion* or your own AS textbook.

The book is organised as follows:

| | | |
|---|---|---|
| **Cognitive psychology: Memory** > | Subsection 1 > | **Topic 1** |
| Developmental psychology: Early social development > | **Subsection 2** > | Topic 2 |
| Research methods > | | Topic 3 |
| Biological psychology: Stress > | | Topic 4 |
| Social psychology: Social influence > | | Topic 5 |
| Individual differences: Psychotherapy (abnormality) > | | |

The AQA specification A AS consists of 6 **modules** (or sections). These are cognitive psychology, developmental psychology, research methods, biological psychology, social psychology and individual differences.

Each module is subdivided into two **subsections**.

In this book, topics have been identified within each subsection. Each **topic** is covered on a *single page*.

In total there are a mere 49 topics!

This book starts with some details about the examination and tips for doing well in the final examination.

| Introduction | > | About this book |
| --- | --- | --- |
| | | The AS exam |
| | | AS exam questions |
| | | How your answers are marked |
| | | A mock exam |
| | | AS exam advice |

## The AS exam

There are two AS exams: Unit 1 (PSYA1) and Unit 2 (PSYA2).

- In each exam all the questions will be compulsory.
- You will have 1½ hours on each paper to answer about 10 questions (some questions are parted).
- The total mark for each paper will be 72 marks.

 ### Unit 1

**Cognitive Psychology, Developmental Psychology and Research Methods**

The exam paper is divided into two sections, each worth 36 marks.

There will be **one** 12 mark extended writing question on this paper. Quality of written communication is assessed in this question.

### Section A – Cognitive Psychology and Research methods

In this section you will be asked questions on the topic of memory, and also be given some brief descriptions of hypothetical studies of memory and asked research methods questions in relation to these hypothetical studies.

### Section B – Developmental Psychology and Research methods

In this section you will be asked questions on the topic of attachment, and again, will be asked research methods questions about hypothetical studies of attachment.

*Psychologists carefully noted the pets' response to the broken water dish.*

 ### Unit 2

**Biological Psychology, Social Psychology and Individual Differences**

This exam paper is divided into three sections, each worth 24 marks.

There will be at least **one** 12 mark extended writing question on this paper. There is no guarantee as to which section it will appear in. Quality of written communication is assessed in this question.

### Section A – Biological Psychology

Most of the questions in this section will be on the topic of stress. Between 4 and 6 marks are likely to be allocated to a question(s) on 'how science works' in relation to stress research.

### Section B – Social Psychology

This follows the same pattern as section A – mainly questions on the topic of social influence, but there are also likely to be between 4 and 6 marks worth of questions on 'how science works', this time related to social influence research.

### Section C – Individual Differences

This also follows the same pattern as section A – mainly questions on the topic of individual differences, plus possibly 4 marks worth of questions on 'how science works', this time related to abnormality.

 ### How science works

The theme 'how science works' is a key feature of the Psychology examination. This includes your knowledge of the methods psychologists use when conducting research, and the advantages/weaknesses of these methods. It also includes the issues of reliability, validity and ethics.

In all areas of the specification you need to be prepared to answer questions related to the topic of 'how science works'.

| Introduction | > | About this book |
| | | The AS exam |
| | | **AS exam questions** |
| | | How your answers are marked |
| | | A mock exam |
| | | AS exam advice |

## AS exam questions

There are various types of question that you are likely to encounter.
We have discussed some of the main ones here.

The authors and publisher wish to thank the Assessment and Qualifications Alliance for AQA examination materials on pages vi and vii.

| Question types | Example | Advice |
|---|---|---|
| **Simple selection question** | The following statements are all related to conformity.<br>**A** Doing what the group does in order to be liked by them.<br>**B** Doing what the group does because we do not know what else to do.<br>**C** Going along with the group, even if we do not really agree with what they are doing.<br>**D** Going along with the group because we accept their beliefs and attitudes into our own cognitions<br>In the table below, write which statement, **A**, **B**, **C**, or **D**, describes each type of conformity.<br><br>| Type of conformity | Statement |<br>| Internalisation | |<br>| Compliance | |<br><br>*(2 marks)*<br>AQA, January 2009 Unit 2 | *Questions like this can sometimes be quite easy and sometimes quite difficult! It is worth taking extra time to make sure you have selected the right answer rather than rushing and throwing away valuable marks.* |
| **Short description question** | What is meant by the term attachment?<br>*(2 marks)*<br>AQA, June 2009 Unit 1<br><br>Cognitive interviews have been developed to improve witness recall. Identify and explain two techniques used in the cognitive interview.<br>*(3 marks + 3 marks)*<br>AQA, June 2009 Unit 1 | *The number of marks available indicates the depth required in your answer.*<br><br>*In this question on cognitive interviews the term 'identify' suggests a simple answer, 'explain' then requires further elaboration.* |
| **Longer description question** | Outline the main features of the multi-store model.<br>*(6 marks)*<br>AQA, January 2009 Unit 1<br><br>What are the implications for social change of research into social influence?<br>*(6 marks)*<br>AQA, January 2009 Unit 2 | *Again, the number of marks available gives you guidance about how much to write. In this question you should avoid including any evaluation, which may not be creditworthy.* |
| **Research studies** | Outline what research has shown about the effects of day care on children's aggressive behaviour.<br>*(6 marks)*<br>AQA, January 2009 Unit 1<br><br>Disruption of attachment can occur when children experience separation from their attachment figure during their early childhood. Outline **one** study of the effects of disruption on attachment.<br>*(4 marks)*<br>AQA, June 2009 Unit 1<br><br>Outline how **one** research study investigated the accuracy of eyewitness testimony (EWT).<br>*(4 marks)*<br>AQA, January 2009 Unit 1 | *There is an important difference between questions that say 'outline research' and those that say 'outline **one** study' – the difference is that in the former case you can describe several studies, whereas in the latter case you will only receive credit for the details of one study.*<br><br>*There is another important difference between the three questions on the left. One question asks about what research has 'shown' whereas the other just asks for an outline of the study. When a question says 'showed', credit will only be given for findings/conclusions. When a question says 'how', credit will only be given for details of procedures. However, when questions just ask for an outline, then procedures/findings/ conclusions are all creditworthy.* |

Introduction

About this book
The AS exam
**AS exam questions**
How your answers are marked
A mock exam
AS exam advice

| Question types | Example | Advice |
|---|---|---|
| **Applying knowledge** | A student teacher finds it very difficult to remember pupils' names. She decides to look in a psychology book to find some useful strategies for improving her memory. Outline **one** strategy the student teacher could use, and explain why this might improve her memory for pupils' names. *(4 marks)* <br> AQA, January 2009 Unit 1 <br><br> In a hospital you are very likely to obey a nurse. However, if you meet her outside the hospital, for example in a shop, you are much less likely to obey. Using your knowledge of how people resist pressures to obey, explain why you are less likely to obey the nurse outside the hospital. *(4 marks)* <br> AQA, January 2009 Unit 2 | *In these questions you will be given an everyday situation and be asked to use your psychological knowledge to provide an informed answer. You must make sure that your answer contains psychological knowledge but at the same time you must make sure you are answering the question.* <br><br> *In the case of the first question on the left, in the examination many students wrote about memory techniques – but didn't explain how these techniques would be used for remembering names.* <br><br> *In the second example, many students just wrote about obedience research and failed to use their knowledge to explain the scenario. Other students said 'you'd obey a nurse because she is in charge' but made no link to psychology.* |
| **Strengths and weaknesses** | Outline **one** limitation of the behavioural approach to psychopathology. *(2 marks)* <br> AQA, June 2009 Unit 2 | *Be guided by the number of marks available and be careful to answer the question – strengths will not be creditworthy, and writing a second limitation would not be creditworthy.* |
| **Differences** | How does the behaviour of securely attached infants differ from that of insecurely attached infants? *(4 marks)* <br> AQA, June 2009 Unit 1 | *Credit will be given for one difference in detail or more than one difference more briefly.* <br><br> *You will only gain credit if you actually identify the difference rather than simply defining the two terms.* |
| **Short essay** | Discuss the emotion-focused approach to coping with stress. *(8 marks)* <br> AQA, January 2009 Unit 2 <br><br> Discuss **one or more** physiological methods of stress management. *(10 marks)* <br> AQA, June 2009 Unit 2 | *The terms 'discuss' or 'outline and evaluate' (or similar) signal that there are marks available for description and evaluation.* <br><br> *These marks are always equal (i.e. 4 + 4 or 5 + 5).* |
| **Long essay (extended writing)** | Outline and evaluate research into the effects of anxiety on the accuracy of eyewitness testimony. *(12 marks)* <br> AQA, June 2009 Unit 1 <br><br> Outline and evaluate **one or more** explanations of why people obey. *(12 marks)* <br> AQA, June 2009 Unit 2 | *The 12 mark extended writing question is marked differently to the other questions. It is marked using the description (AO1) and evaluation (AO2) criteria shown on the following page.* |
| **Research methods** | You will be given a description of a study and then a number of short questions such as: <br> **a** What is the dependent variable in this study? *(2 marks)* <br> **b** What experimental design was used in this study? *(1 mark)* <br> **c** Explain **one** strength of this experimental design in the context of this study. *(2 marks)* | *This type of research methods question only appears on Unit 1.* <br><br> *Some of the questions require contextualisation, i.e. you only get full credit if you display your psychological knowledge and apply this to the study described in the exam question. For example, for part (c) you would need to identify one strength and then say why it is a strength in this particular study.* |
| **How science works** | How have psychologists investigated the relationship between stress and the immune system? *(4 marks)* <br> AQA, January 2009 Unit 2 <br><br> **a** Milgram's work can be criticised for being unethical. Describe **one** way in which his work is unethical. *(2 marks)* <br> **b** Apart from ethical issues, give **one** strength and **one** limitation of Milgram's methodology. *(2 marks + 2 marks)* <br> AQA, January 2009 Unit 2 | *On both Units 1 and 2 questions appear on 'how science works', i.e. questions about the methods psychologists use when conducting research, the advantages/weaknesses of these methods as well as issues of reliability, validity and ethics.* |

Introduction                    > About this book
                                  The AS exam
                                  AS exam questions
                                  **How your answers are marked**
                                  A mock exam
                                  AS exam advice

# How your answers are marked

 ## Assessment objectives

There are three assessment objectives in AS exam questions:

**AO1** description

For example, 'Outline the multi-store model' requires a description of the model.

**AO2** evaluation and application of knowledge

For example, 'Give **one** strength of the multi-store model' requires you to provide some evaluation of the model.

Or 'Suggest **two** strategies that Sanjay could use when revising' requires you to apply your knowledge.

**AO3** Design, conduct and report research

For example 'Explain why the researcher might have chosen to use a volunteer sample' requires you to demonstrate your understanding of the research process.

In general, you do not actually need to worry about these assessment objectives – you just simply answer the exam questions.

**The only time you do need to think AO1 and AO2 is for the essay-style questions.**

- These questions start with the word 'Discuss' or 'Describe and evaluate'.
- This means you need to provide description (AO1) and evaluation (AO2) in equal measure.
- These questions are worth more than other questions – perhaps 8 marks or 12 marks.
- These questions are likely to be marked used the mark scheme shown below.

 ## How marks are awarded

In general, marks are awarded for detail and elaboration. The main difference between a good answer and a weak answer is the amount of *detail* (in AO1 answers) and *elaboration* (in AO2 answers). See page xii for advice about how to improve the detail and elaboration of your answers.

## Abbreviated mark scheme for 12 mark questions

| | Description (AO1 – assessment objective 1) | | | |
|---|---|---|---|---|
| **Marks** | **Detail** | **Knowledge and understanding** | **Selection of appropriate material** | **Presentation of information** |
| 6 | Accurate and reasonably detailed | Sound | Appropriate | Clear and coherent |
| 5–4 | Generally accurate, less detailed | Relevant | Some evidence | Appropriate |
| 3–2 | Basic | Some relevant | Little evidence | Appropriate |
| 1 | Very brief/flawed | Very little | Largely or wholly inappropriate | |

| | Evaluation (AO2 – assessment objective 2) | | |
|---|---|---|---|
| **Marks** | **Use of material** | **Range of issues and/or evidence** | **Expression of ideas , specialist terms, spelling, etc.** |
| 6 | Effective | Broad range in reasonable depth or narrower range in greater depth | Clear and good range, few errors |
| 5–4 | Not always effective | Range in limited depth or narrower range in greater depth | Reasonable, some errors |
| 3–2 | Basic | Superficial consideration of restricted range | Lacks clarity, some specialist terms, errors |
| 1 | Rudimentary | Just discernible | Poor, few specialist terms |

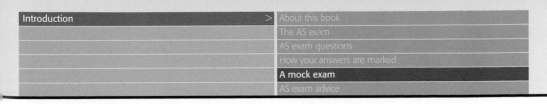

| Introduction | > About this book |
| --- | --- |
| | The AS exam |
| | AS exam questions |
| | How your answers are marked |
| | A mock exam |
| | AS exam advice |

## A mock exam

We have written two mock exams for you to try, one for each unit exam. When you have revised the content of each unit you should answer the questions under timed exam conditions. Suggested answers can be found on our website www.folensblogs.com/psychcompanion/blog/.

## PSYA 1 Mock exam

Time allowed: 1 hour and 30 minutes.

The marks for questions are shown in brackets.

Question 10 should be answered in continuous prose.

### SECTION A: COGNITIVE PSYCHOLOGY AND RESEARCH METHODS

Answer **all** questions.

1   The working memory model consists of several components, some of which are listed below.

   **A**   The central executive

   **B**   The phonological store

   **C**   The articulatory process

   **D**   The visuo-spatial sketchpad

   Copy the table below, and fill in the letter for the component which matches each description.

| Description | Component |
| --- | --- |
| 1. Modality free system which assigns tasks to other components. | |
| 2. Acts like an inner voice, repeating words that are heard. | |
| 3. Stores information about sounds. | |
| 4. Used, for example, when counting how many windows there are on your house. | |

*(4 marks)*

2   The multi-store model of memory was one of the first explanations suggested for how memory is organised but it is no longer considered an appropriate model for understanding memory.

   **a**   Explain **one** reason why the multi-store model is no longer well-respected by psychologists.   *(4 marks)*

   **b**   Outline **one** strength of the multi-store model.   *(2 marks)*

3   Short-term memory and long-term memory can be contrasted in terms of capacity, duration and encoding.

   **a**   Give a detailed description of the capacity of short-term memory.   *(3 marks)*

   **b**   Describe how psychologists have investigated encoding processes in memory.   *(4 marks)*

   **c**   Explain **one or more** problems that have been encountered when conducting such research.   *(4 marks)*

4   The primary school in a small village is located right next to the village shop. School children inevitably call in to the shop on their way home from school to buy sweets. On one day, a group of 10-year-old children were in the shop when an armed raid took place. The children were interviewed separately by the police about the identity of the men who raided the shop.

   **a**   Explain why the children might not be good eyewitnesses. Refer to psychological research in your answer.   *(3 marks)*

   **b**   The police decided to use elements of the cognitive interview when talking to the children. Select **one** element of the cognitive interview and explain how this might have been used with the children.   *(3 marks)*

   **c**   Explain why the use of this element of the cognitive interview might have been effective.   *(3 marks)*

5   A group of psychology students have been studying strategies to improve memory and decide to conduct some research themselves to see which strategy works best for revision. They select two strategies and give each student two pieces of work to learn. The students are instructed to use Strategy 1 to learn the first piece of work and Strategy 2 for the second piece of work.

   **a**   Identify the experimental design used in this study.   *(1 mark)*

   **b**   Give **one** disadvantage of using this design in this study.   *(2 marks)*

   **c**   Explain how you might overcome this disadvantage.   *(3 marks)*

Continued on next page

| Introduction | > | About this book |
| --- | --- | --- |
| | | The AS exam |
| | | AS exam questions |
| | | How your answers are marked |
| | | **A mock exam** |
| | | AS exam advice |

## SECTION B: DEVELOPMENTAL PSYCHOLOGY AND RESEARCH METHODS

Answer **all** questions.

6   **a**   Identify **one** cultural variation in attachment. *(1 mark)*

   **b**   Explain why this variation might occur in different cultures. *(3 marks)*

7   Bowlby developed a theory of attachment based on the evolutionary perspective.

   **a**   Briefly outline the key elements of the evolutionary perspective. *(3 marks)*

   **b**   Outline **one** study that has been used as support for Bowlby's theory of attachment. *(4 marks)*

8   A number of studies have found that children who attend day care for more than 30 hours per week are more aggressive when they arrive at school. Dr Patel has decided to compare results found in America with day care centres in urban areas of India. For this study two items of data were collected for each child:

   •   The number of hours they spent on average in day care per week. (Children who did not attend day care were excluded from the study).

   •   A score for aggressiveness based on teachers' rating of each child.

   **a**   Identify the co-variables in this study. *(2 marks)*

   **b**   This study is looking at a correlation between two variables. Explain why you might expect to find a positive correlation between the variables. *(2 marks)*

   **c**   Explain **one** weakness of a study using a correlational analysis. *(2 marks)*

   **d**   Identify **one** ethical issue that might arise in this study and explain how you would deal with it. *(4 marks)*

9   David is doing his work experience at a day nursery. At the end of each day he notices that some of the children greet their parents enthusiastically whereas other children seem quite shy and sometimes even ignore their parents.

   Using your knowledge of attachment types, explain why such differences may occur. *(3 marks)*

10   Outline and evaluate research into the effects of institutionalisation. *(12 marks)*

## PSYA 2 Mock exam

Time allowed: 1 hour and 30 minutes.

The marks for questions are shown in brackets.

Question 3 should be answered in continuous prose.

## SECTION A: BIOLOGICAL PSYCHOLOGY

Answer **all** questions.

1   People develop various strategies to cope with stress in their lives. Some of these strategies are emotion-focused and some are problem-focused.

   **a**   Outline **one** emotion-focused strategy that can be used to cope with stress. *(4 marks)*

   **b**   Explain the difference between emotion-focused and problem-focused ways of coping with stress. *(4 marks)*

2   Some psychologists have suggested that daily hassles are an important source of stress.

   How have psychologists investigated the relationship between daily hassles and stress? *(4 marks)*

3   'Some people are more adversely affected by stress than others'.

   Outline and evaluate the role of personality factors in stress. *(12 marks)*

Continued on next page

| Introduction | > | About this book |
| | | The AS exam |
| | | AS exam questions |
| | | How your answers are marked |
| | | **A mock exam** |
| | | AS exam advice |

## SECTION B: SOCIAL PSYCHOLOGY
Answer **all** questions.

4  Kayla and Jasmine are close friends and go to the same school. One of their teachers arranged for a speaker to come to the school to talk to the students about animal rights. After the talk, the speaker offered the students a chance to join his organisation and virtually everyone wanted to join, including Kayla and Jasmine. A few weeks later, Jasmine confided that she just joined because everyone else had. This surprised Kayla because she felt really committed to the cause and had volunteered to help out at a fundraising event.

    **a**  With reference to the example above, explain the concepts of 'internalisation' and 'compliance'.
*(3 marks + 3 marks)*

    **b**  Outline how **one** research study has investigated the effects of conformity.
*(4 marks)*

5  Milgram's research into obedience has been criticised in terms of lacking validity.
Describe and evaluate the validity of Milgram's research on obedience.
*(8 marks)*

6  A lot of research into social influence suggests that people are highly conformist and obedient. But research also shows that people can be independent in their behaviour.

    **a**  Outline **one** explanation of how people resist pressures to conform.
*(3 marks)*

    **b**  Outline **one** explanation of how people resist pressures to obey authority.
*(3 marks)*

## SECTION C: INDIVIDUAL DIFFERENCES
Answer **all** questions.

7  The following statements are related to definitions of abnormality. Write down the letters that represent the **three** statements related to the 'deviation from social norms' definition.

    **A**  Deviance is related to context and degree.

    **B**  Abnormality is judged in terms of not being able to cope.

    **C**  Abnormality is shown by a deviance from social standards.

    **D**  The definition is open to abuse because norms vary across time and situation.

    **E**  Mastery of the environment is an important criteria.
*(3 marks)*

8  Describe the key features of the psychodynamic model of abnormality.
*(4 marks)*

9  Daniel has been having difficulty sleeping since he lost his job. He has also lost all enthusiasm for life and can't motivate himself to do anything. He went to see his doctor about his problems and discussed various options including biological and psychological therapies.

    **a**  Daniel's doctor thought psychological therapies might be a better option. Outline **one** argument the doctor might use to convince Daniel that psychological therapies are better than biological ones.
*(3 marks)*

    **b**  The doctor thinks that Cognitive Behavioural Therapy might be the best psychological therapy. Suggest how he might explain the main techniques involved in this therapy to Daniel.
*(4 marks)*

    **c**  Daniel asks whether there are any drawbacks to using Cognitive Behavioural Therapy. What would you tell him?
*(3 marks)*

10  Psychologists conduct research to assess the effectiveness of any method used to treat abnormality.

    **a**  Describe how psychologists have investigated the effectiveness of drugs in treating abnormality.
*(3 marks)*

    **b**  Describe ethical issues that may arise when conducting research on the use of drugs to treat abnormality.
*(4 marks)*

Introduction | > | About this book
| | | The AS exam
| | | AS exam questions
| | | How your answers are marked
| | | A mock exam
| | | AS exam advice

# AS exam advice

## Writing good answers

###  Detailed description

If a question says 'identify' then you know a single word or phrase will usually be sufficient for your answer. But if the question says 'describe', 'outline or 'explain' then you must provide some further information. Consider this question and answer:

*Question*: 'Describe **one** reason why people obey'.

*Answer*: 'Because it is justified'.

The answer, so far, is only worth one mark and needs more detail to attract further credit. You could add detail by:

- **Providing an example**: 'People obey because it is justified, for example during the Holocaust, Nazi propaganda portrayed the Jews as a danger to all Germans, thus justifying the horrific obedience that was to follow'.

- **Adding a study**: 'People obey because it is justified. This was shown in Milgram's study of obedience to authority, where participants were given the initial justification of their role in delivering electric shocks that science wanted to help people improve their memory through the use of reward and punishment'.

###  Elaboration in essays

The main difference between a weak essay and a good essay is the amount of *detail* (AO1) and *elaboration* (for AO2).

For good elaboration you should use the **three point rule**:

1 **Identify** your AO2 point (e.g. criticism, application, individual difference, etc.)

2 **Justify** it (what evidence do you have for this?)

3 **Elaborate** it (how does this affect the topic being evaluated? Is this good or bad for it and why?)

For example, if your criticism of a study is 'lack of ecological validity' then you have identified it. You need to justify your claim in the particular study (e.g. studies of this phenomenon in other settings haven't produced the same results). Finally, you need to indicate why ecological validity is a problem in this study (e.g. this means that we can't generalise from the original study to other settings, which limits its explanatory usefulness).

## Effective revision

- **Get yourself motivated** – People do better when they are highly motivated. Don't expect someone else to motivate you (the draw of £50 for exam success) … think of your own reason why you really really want to do well.

- **Revisit regularly** – Knowledge that is not used regularly becomes less immediately accessible. The trick, therefore, is to review what you have learned at regular intervals. Each time you review material, it will take less time and will pay dividends later on!

- **Short bursts are best** – As you probably know all too well, your attention is prone to wander after a relatively short period of time. Research findings suggest that 30–45 minutes at a time is best. What should you do when your attention begins to wander? As a rule, the greater the physiological change (i.e. go for a walk rather than surfing the Internet), the more refreshed you will be when returning for your next 30–45 minute stint.

- **Be multi-sensory** – Why stick to using just one of your senses when revising? Visual learners learn best by seeing what they are learning, so make the most of text, diagrams, graphs, etc. By contrast, auditory learners learn best by listening (and talking), taking in material using their sense of hearing. You may associate more with one of these styles than the other, but actually we can make use of many different types of learning styles. As well as *reading* your notes and *looking* at pictures and diagrams, try *listening* to your notes and *talking* about topics with other people, and even *performing* some of the material such as role playing a study.

## Exam stress

A moderate level of stress is good for performance but too much can impair your ability to recall information and use it effectively in the exam. A wise student learns to control their stress *before* the examination, and makes frequent use of stress management even during the revision stage.

One interesting fact is that physical activity (e.g. stretching your arms or feet) reduces stress because the activity tells the body that the stressor has been dealt with and, therefore, the sympathetic nervous system can 'stand down', putting you in a more relaxed state.

# Chapter 1

# Cognitive psychology

Column 1: tick when you have produced brief notes.

Column 2: tick when you have a good grasp of this topic.

Column 3: tick during the final revision when you feel you have complete mastery of the topic.

| Key terms • 3 marks worth of material | 1 | 2 | 3 |
|---|---|---|---|
| Short-term memory (STM) | | | |
| Long-term memory (LTM) | | | |
| Encoding | | | |
| Duration | | | |
| Capacity | | | |
| Eyewitness testimony (EWT) | | | |
| Misleading information | | | |
| **Research studies related to …** • **6 marks worth of description** • **6 marks worth of evaluation (including the issues of reliability, validity and ethics)** | | | |
| STM | | | |
| LTM | | | |
| Capacity | | | |
| Duration | | | |
| Encoding | | | |
| Multi-store model | | | |
| Working memory model | | | |
| Accuracy of EWT | | | |
| Effect of age of witness on EWT | | | |
| Effect of anxiety on EWT | | | |
| Effect of misleading questions in EWT | | | |
| Cognitive interview | | | |
| Strategies for memory improvement | | | |
| **Factors that affect …** • **6 marks worth of material** | | | |
| Capacity of STM | | | |
| Duration of STM | | | |
| Encoding in STM and LTM | | | |
| Accuracy of eyewitness testimony | | | |
| **Explanations/theories** • **6 marks worth of description** • **6 marks worth of evaluation (both strengths and weaknesses)** | | | |
| Multi-store model | | | |
| Working memory model | | | |
| **Applications of memory research** • **6 marks worth of material** | | | |
| Strategies for memory improvement | | | |

| Cognitive psychology: Memory | > | Models of memory | > | Nature of memory |
| Developmental psychology: Early social development | > | Memory in everyday life | > | Multi-store model of memory |
| Research methods | > | | | Working memory model |
| Biological psychology: Stress | > | | | |
| Social psychology: Social influence | > | | | |
| Individual differences: Psychotherapy (abnormality) | > | | | |

## KEY TERMS

### Capacity
- A measure of how much can be held in memory.
- Measured in terms of bits of information, such as number of digits.

### Duration
- A measure of how long a memory lasts before it is no longer available.

### Encoding
- The way information is changed so it can be stored in memory.
- Information enters the brain via the senses (e.g. eyes and ears) and is then stored in various forms, such as visual codes (like a picture), acoustic forms (sounds), or a semantic form (the meaning of the experience).

### Long-term memory (LTM)
- Memory for events that have happened in the past.
- Lasts anywhere from 2 minutes to 100 years.
- Potentially unlimited duration and capacity.

### Short-term memory (STM)
- Memory for immediate events.
- Lasts for a very short time and disappears unless it is rehearsed.
- Limited duration and limited capacity.
- Sometimes referred to as *working memory*.

| | STM | LTM |
|---|---|---|
| Duration | Measured in seconds and minutes | Measured in hours, days and years |
| Capacity | Less than 7 chunks | Potentially unlimited |
| Encoding | Acoustic (i.e. information represented as sounds) or visual | Semantic (i.e. information represented by its meaning) |

## Duration of STM

 keySTUDY Peterson and Peterson (1959)

**How?** Method – **lab experiment**. Participants: 24 students. Participants were given a **nonsense trigram** to be remembered and also given a three-digit number. They were asked to count backwards from the number until told to stop and recall the nonsense trigram. This was repeated eight times with different retention intervals: 3, 6, 9, 12, 15, or 18 seconds.

**Showed?** Participants could remember about 90% when there was only a 3 second interval, which dropped to about 20% after 9 seconds and about 2% when there was an 18 second interval. This suggests that STM has a duration of less than 18 seconds if verbal rehearsal is prevented. In fact, much information has disappeared within a few seconds.

**Evaluation** (1) **Ecological validity**: the stimulus material is artificial and therefore findings may not apply to all aspects of everyday life, though it does apply to memorising verbal material. (2) **Internal validity**: were they testing duration? Trigrams may have been displaced by numbers when counting backwards and therefore forgetting was not due to spontaneous **decay** but, instead, due to **displacement**.

 ResearchUPDATE Nairne *et al.* (1999)

**How?** Participants were asked to recall the *same* items across trials, whereas in the earlier study different items were used on each trial, which would have led to interference between items, decreasing recall.

**Showed?** Items could be recalled after as long as 96 seconds. Therefore it seems that information remains for quite a while in STM *unless* other material replaces or overwrites it.

## Duration of LTM

 ResearchEVIDENCE

**Shepard** conducted a **lab experiment** to test the duration of LTM. He showed participants 612 memorable pictures, one at a time. An hour later they were shown some of these pictures within a set of others and displayed almost perfect recognition. Four months later they were still able to recognise 50% of the photographs.

**Bahrick *et al.*** conducted a **natural experiment**. They asked people of various ages to put names to faces from their high school year book and 48 years on, people were about 70% accurate. In this case, the material to be remembered was more meaningful to the participants and therefore the duration of the long-term memories was better.

Capacity and encoding covered on facing page.

| Cognitive psychology: Memory | > | Models of memory | > | Nature of memory |
| Developmental psychology: Early social development | > | Memory in everyday life | > | Multi-store model of memory |
| Research methods | > | | | Working memory model |
| Biological psychology: Stress | > | | | |
| Social psychology: Social influence | > | | | |
| Individual differences: Psychotherapy (abnormality) | > | | | |

## KEY TERMS

### Chunking

- Miller proposed that the capacity of STM can be enhanced by grouping sets of digits or letters into meaningful units or 'chunks'.
- For example it is easier to remember 100 1000 10 10000 than 10010001010000.
- Miller suggested we can remember 7 ± 2 chunks at a time.
- The size of a chunk may affect how many other chunks can be processed.

### Digit span technique

- A technique to assess the span of immediate (short-term) memory.
- Participants are given progressively more digits in a list to see how many can be recalled.

## Capacity of STM

 ResearchEVIDENCE

**Miller** reviewed previous research and concluded that the span of **STM** is 7 ± 2, e.g. people can cope reasonably well with counting seven dots flashed onto a screen but not many more than this.

**Jacobs** used the **digit span technique** to assess the capacity of STM. He found the average span for digits was 9.3 items, whereas it was 7.3 for letters. It may be easier to recall digits because there are only 10 possible digits (0–9) wheras there are 26 letters.

Jacobs also found that digit span increased with age; 8-year-olds could remember an average of 6.6 digits, whereas the mean for 19-year-olds was 8.6 digits. This might be due to a gradual increase in brain capacity, and/or that people develop strategies to improve their digit span, such as **chunking**.

 Chunking

**Miller** also found that people can recall 5 *words* as well as they can recall 5 *letters* – we **chunk** things together and then can remember more.

**Simon** conducted a **lab experiment**. He found that the size of the chunk matters – people had a shorter span for larger chunks, such as 8-word phrases, than smaller chunks, such as one-syllable words.

**Cowan** reviewed a variety of studies on the capacity of STM and concluded that STM is likely to be limited to about 4 chunks.

**RealWORLD application** – **Baddeley** discovered that if the initial letters of a postcode were meaningful (e.g. BS for Bristol) it made the postcode easier to remember. Numbers were best remembered if they were placed between the city name and random letters.

## Encoding in STM and LTM

 keySTUDY Baddeley (1966)

**How?** Method – **lab experiment**. Participants were given lists of acoustically similar or dissimilar words and semantically similar or dissimilar words.

**Showed?** Participants had more difficulty remembering acoustically similar words in STM but not in LTM, whereas semantically similar words posed little problem for short-term recall but led to muddled long-term memories.

 otherRESEARCH

**Brandimote et al.** conducted a **lab experiment**. They found that participants used visual encoding in STM if they were given a *visual* task (pictures) and were prevented from doing any *verbal* rehearsal in the retention interval (they had to say 'la la la') before performing a *visual* recall task. Normally we 'translate' visual images into verbal codes in STM, but since verbal rehearsal was prevented, they used visual codes.

**Wickens et al.** found that STM sometimes uses a semantic code rather than being restricted to acoustic coding.

In LTM **Frost** showed that recall was related to visual as well as semantic categories. **Nelson and Rothbart** found evidence of acoustic coding in LTM.

## PUTTING IT ALL TOGETHER

Research supports a distinction between STM and LTM in terms of duration (less than 18 seconds or forever), capacity (less than 7 chunks or infinite) and encoding (*generally* acoustic or semantic).

| Cognitive psychology: Memory | > | Models of memory | > | Nature of memory |
| Developmental psychology: Early social development | > | Memory in everyday life | > | **Multi-store model of memory** |
| Research methods | > | | | Working memory model |
| Biological psychology: Stress | > | | | |
| Social psychology: Social influence | > | | | |
| Individual differences: Psychotherapy (abnormality) | > | | | |

## KEY TERMS

### Multi-store model (MSM)
- An explanation of memory.
- Based on three separate memory stores.
- And how information is transferred between these stores.

### Sensory memory (SM)
- Information at the senses – information collected by your eyes, ears, nose, fingers and so on.
- Information is retained for a very brief period by the sensory registers (less than half a second).
- Capacity of sensory memory is very large.
- Method of encoding depends on the sense organ involved, i.e. visual for the eyes, acoustic for the ears.

▲ *The multi-store model*

### ⟳ PUTTING IT ALL TOGETHER

Research does support the view that there are a number of different memory stores which are quantitatively and qualitatively different, as described by the multi-store model. However the multi-store model is oversimplified.

# Multi-store model (Atkinson and Shiffrin, 1968)

- An explanation of how memory processes work based on the idea that there are three separate stores (**SM**, **STM**, **LTM**).
- Each store has unique characteristics: **duration**, **capacity** and **encoding**.
- Information first arrives at SM. Attention causes transference to STM.
- Information in STM is in a fragile state, and disappears if not rehearsed (**decay**) or if new information enters (**displacement**).
- Increasing rehearsal leads to transfer from STM to LTM; the more rehearsal of an item the better it is remembered.
- Rehearsal is maintenance rehearsal (verbal) but also elaborative rehearsal.

## ⬡ Research**EVIDENCE** supporting the MSM

**Sensory memory – Sperling** conducted a **lab experiment**. He asked participants to report 12 letters/digits from a three line display after a 50 millisecond delay. Recall was poorer for all items (5 items recalled, about 42%) than when asked to give one row only (3 items recalled, 75%). This shows that information decays rapidly in the sensory store.

**Serial position effect – Glanzer and Cunitz** conducted a **lab experiment**. They gave participants a list of words and found that words recalled tended to be from the start of the list (**primacy effect**) and end of list (**recency effect**). This **serial position effect** occurs because the first words are best rehearsed and transferred to LTM, and the last words are in STM when you start recalling the list.

**Brain scans – Beardsley** used **brain scanning** to investigate brain activity and found that the **prefrontal cortex** is active during STM tasks. **Squire et al.** also used **brain scanning** and found the **hippocampus** is active when LTM is engaged. This shows there are distinct stores.

**Case study of HM – Scoville and Milner** conducted a **case study**. They found that the ability to form new LTM was impaired when the hippocampus was removed; LTMs formed prior to the operation remained intact.

## ⬡ Evaluation

### Strengths
1. **Research support** e.g. studies above and on previous pages related to duration, capacity, encoding.
2. **Produces testable predictions**, which is important for the scientific process to enable theory testing and verification.

### Limitations
1. **STM and LTM are not unitary stores**. STM has verbal and visual stores (see WMM on facing page) and LTM is divided into semantic, episodic and procedural memory as well as perceptual-representation system (PRS). Supported by **Spiers et al.** who studied amnesiac patients, whose procedural and PRS systems were intact but not the other types of LTM.
2. **Rehearsal involves processing (elaboration)** as well as maintenance. Supported by **Craik and Tulving** who found that words processed more deeply (semantically) were better remembered.
3. **STM not entirely separate from LTM**. **Ruchkin et al.** found participants' brain activity was different when they processed real or pseudo-words.

| Cognitive psychology: Memory | > | Models of memory | > | Nature of memory |
| Developmental psychology: Early social development | > | Memory in everyday life | > | Multi-store model of memory |
| Research methods | > | | | Working memory model |
| Biological psychology: Stress | > | | | |
| Social psychology: Social influence | > | | | |
| Individual differences: Psychotherapy (abnormality) | > | | | |

## KEY TERMS

### Central executive
- Monitors and coordinates all other mental functions in WM.

### Episodic buffer
- Receives input from many sources.
- Temporarily stores this information.
- Integrates it in order to construct a mental episode of what is being experienced right now.

### Phonological loop
- Encodes speech sounds.
- Involves maintenance rehearsal (repeating the words over and over again i.e. a *loop*).
- Divided into **phonological store** (inner ear) and **articulatory process** (inner voice).

### Visuo-spatial sketchpad
- Encodes visual information.
- Divided into the **visual cache** (stores information) and **inner scribe** (spatial relations).

### Word-length effect
- People remember lists of short words better than long words.
- Governed by the capacity of the phonological loop.

### Working memory model (WMM)
- An explanation of STM, called 'working memory'.
- Based on four components, some with storage capacity.

---

 **PUTTING IT ALL TOGETHER**

The working memory model offers a refinement of the multi-store model, describing working memory in terms of specialised auditory and visual units.

---

# Working memory model (Baddeley and Hitch, 1974)

- An explanation of STM (i.e. the memory used when working on something, such as solving problems, comprehending language, etc.).
- **Central executive** is an attentional process to monitor incoming data and allocate 'slave systems' to tasks. Has very limited capacity.
- **Phonological loop** deals with auditory information and preserves its order. Subdivided into **phonological store**, which stores the words you hear, and **articulatory process**, which allows maintenance rehearsal – repeating the words.
- **Visuo-spatial sketchpad** stores visual and/or spatial information. Subdivided into **visual cache**, which stores visual data, and **inner scribe**, which encodes the arrangement of objects in the visual field.
- **Episodic buffer** provides a temporary store and links with LTM.

##  Research**EVIDENCE** supporting the WMM

**Dual task performance – Hitch and Baddeley** conducted a **lab experiment**. They demonstrated that performance was slower when participants were given a task involving the central executive and a second task involving both the central executive and the articulatory loop, than articulatory loop alone or no extra task.

**Phonological loop – Baddeley *et al.*** conducted a **lab experiment**. They demonstrated that the phonological loop holds the amount of information you can say in 2 seconds, but the **word length effect** disappears if a person is given an **articulatory suppression task** (a repetitive task that ties up the articulatory process). This is evidence of the phonological loop (because there is a finite space for rehearsal related to what can be said) and the articulatory suppression task is evidence of the articulatory process.

**Visuo-spatial sketchpad – Baddeley *et al.*** conducted a **lab experiment**. They showed that participants had more difficulty doing two visual tasks (track a light and describe letter F) than a visual and verbal task.

**Case studies – Shallice and Warrington** conducted a **case study** of KF whose LTM was intact, as was STM for visual stimuli, but he had poor STM ability with verbal material (letters and digits but not sounds).

## Evaluation

### Strengths
1. **Emphasises process** more than the MSM and presents a more detailed understanding of STM.
2. **Plenty of research support** for different stores and dual-task performance, as described above.
3. **Produces testable** predictions, which is important for the scientific process.

### Limitations
1. **Central executive is vaguely defined** and doesn't really explain anything. May consist of separate components.
2. **Evidence from brain-damaged patients may not be reliable** because it concerns unique cases often involving traumatic experiences.
3. **The WMM is restricted to STM** and has nothing to say about LTM.

| Cognitive psychology: Memory | > | Models of memory | > | Eyewitness testimony |
| Developmental psychology: Early social development | > | Memory in everyday life | > | Cognitive interview |
| Research methods | > | | | Strategies for memory improvement |
| Biological psychology: Stress | > | | | |
| Social psychology: Social influence | > | | | |
| Individual differences: Psychotherapy (abnormality) | > | | | |

## The effect of misleading information on EWT

 **keySTUDY** Loftus and Palmer (1974)

**1st experiment, how?** Method – **lab experiment**. Forty-five students were shown films of traffic accidents. **Leading questions** afterwards included a critical one about speed of car containing the word 'hit', 'smashed', 'collided', 'bumped' or 'contacted'.

**Showed?** The group with 'smashed' estimated a higher speed, the group given the word 'contacted' estimated the lowest speed (see graph on right). Suggests that leading questions (**post-event information**) can have a significant effect on memory (could be on how memory is stored or how it is retrieved).

**2nd experiment** to investigate whether post-event information alters storage or retrieval. A different set of participants were shown a film of an accident. A week later they asked whether there was any broken glass.

**Showed?** Those given the question with 'smashed' were more likely to recollect broken glass (there was none) (see graph on right). Shows that post-event information affects initial storage.

**Evaluation** (1) **Validity** – not true to life because participants may not take the task seriously and thus behaviour does not represent real EWT; **Foster et al.** showed that recall is more accurate in real life. (2) **Demand characteristic** – very hard to estimate speed so participants use any available clue, in this case the verb in the question.

 otherRESEARCH

**Loftus et al.** conducted a **lab experiment**. Participants were shown photos of a car at a junction with a STOP or YIELD sign, then asked questions either consistent with a photo (e.g. participant saw photo of a STOP sign and asked about a car at a STOP sign), or inconsistent (e.g. participants saw photo of a YIELD sign but asked about a car at a STOP sign). Finally, they were shown pairs of photos and asked to identify which was one of the original photos. Those given inconsistent questions (i.e. misleading) were 41% correct in their identification, compared with 75% when consistent questions were used.

**Bekerian and Bowers** disputed the above result. When participants were given a question that matched the sign they were shown (STOP or YIELD) their recall was more accurate when questions were consistent than inconsistent. *But* when the slides were presented in the right sequence, misleading information (inconsistent question) had no effect. This suggests that misleading questions (post-event information) affect retrieval rather than storage.

 Evaluation

**RealWORLD application – Wells and Olsen** reported that mistaken eyewitness identification was the largest single factor in convicting innocent people. Psychological research has been crucial in providing a scientific understanding of how misleading information may affect EWT.

**IndividualDIFFERENCES** (1) **Gender** – men and women take an interest in different aspects of a scene but both are equally accurate (**Wells and Olsen**). (2) **Age** – elderly people are less able to remember the source of information than younger people (**Schacter et al.**).

| Verb | Mean speed estimate |
| --- | --- |
| Smashed | 40.8 |
| Collided | 39.3 |
| Bumped | 38.1 |
| Hit | 34 |
| Contracted | 31.8 |

▲ *Findings from 1st experiment by Loftus and Palmer*

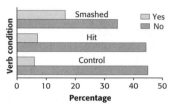

▲ *Findings from 2nd experiment by Loftus and Palmer*

### KEY TERMS

**Eyewitness testimony (EWT)**
- The evidence provided in court by a person who witnessed a crime, with a view to identifying the perpetrator of the crime.
- The accuracy of eyewitness recall may be affected during initial encoding, subsequent storage and eventual retrieval.

**Leading (misleading) question**
- A question that, either by its form or content, suggests to the witness what answer is desired, or leads him to the desired answer.

**Post-event information**
- Information given to a witness after the event.
- Such as a leading question.

More on EWT on facing page.

| Cognitive psychology: Memory | > | Models of memory | > | Eyewitness testimony |
| Developmental psychology: Early social development | > | Memory in everyday life | > | Cognitive interview |
| Research methods | > | | | Strategies for memory improvement |
| Biological psychology: Stress | > | | | |
| Social psychology: Social influence | > | | | |
| Individual differences: Psychotherapy (abnormality) | > | | | |

## KEY TERMS

### Anxiety

- A nervous emotional state where we fear that something unpleasant is about to happen.
- People often become anxious when they are in stressful situations.
- Anxiety tends to be accompanied by physiological arousal (e.g. a pounding heart and rapid shallow breathing). Therefore research in this area is often focused on the effects of arousal.

## The effect of anxiety on EWT

###  ResearchEVIDENCE

**Deffenbacher et al.** conducted a **meta-analysis**. They analysed 18 studies of anxiety and EWT. Many showed that stress has a negative impact on accuracy of EWT but some studies showed that anxiety may actually enhance the accuracy of recall.

**Christianson and Hubinette** conducted a **questionnaire**. They spoke to 58 real witnesses to bank robberies. The greater the threat, the more accurate the recall and the more detail was remembered, compared to onlookers who were less emotionally aroused.

**Johnson and Scott** conducted a **lab experiment** to demonstrate the **weapon focus effect** – arousal (anxiety) may focus attention on central features of a crime (e.g. the weapon) and thus reduce recall for details (e.g. of perpetrator's face). In this experiment, a man runs through a room carrying a pen covered in grease or knife covered in blood. Witnesses were 49% accurate in identifying the man with the pen, compared to 33% accuracy with the knife.

##  Evaluation

**Contradictory findings can be explained** in terms of the **Yerkes-Dodson law** – medium levels of arousal (anxiety) enhance accurate recall, whereas high levels decrease it.

**RealWORLD application – Rinolo et al.** used evidence from the sinking of the Titanic, where 75% of the survivors had reported that the ship broke apart when sinking. Their testimony was regarded as inaccurate until the wreck was discovered and their account was proved right. This supports the view that anxiety does not necessarily result in inaccurate recall.

## The effect of age on EWT

###  ResearchEVIDENCE

The following studies are all **natural or quasi-experiments** because the IV (age) varies naturally.

**Brassard** found that young children (four years old) were more affected by cues from the interviewer than were slightly older children (eight years old).

**Parker and Carranza** found that primary school children were more likely to choose someone from a mock line-up than adults, but also more likely to make errors.

**Yarney** found that older adults (45–65) were less confident, but not less accurate, when recalling a confederate than younger adults.

**Memon et al.** found that accuracy in older people (60–82) dropped when the identification task was delayed for a week.

**Anastasi and Rhodes** found that young (18–25) and middle-aged (35–45) participants were significantly more accurate in recall of target faces than older (55–78) participants.

##  Evaluation

**Own-age bias** – Apparent superior performance of younger people may be because the faces to be recognised are younger faces. **Anastasi and Rhodes** found that all age groups are most accurate when the target photographs are from their own age group.

**Explaining own-age bias** – The less contact we have with certain groups of people, the poorer our ability to discriminate between individuals in this group (= **differential experience hypothesis**, Brigham and Malpas).

**ResearchMETHODS** – Participants may not behave as they would in everyday life in contrived studies. They may not take the task as seriously as in real life or, on the other hand, they may be looking for cues in an experiment which they wouldn't do in everyday life.

---

### ⟳ PUTTING IT ALL TOGETHER

Eyewitness testimony may lack accuracy in some situations, e.g. because of misleading questions, high arousal or identifying people of a different age group. However it may also be impressively accurate.

| Cognitive psychology: Memory | > | Models of memory | > | Eyewitness testimony |
| Developmental psychology: Early social development | > | Memory in everyday life | > | Cognitive interview |
| Research methods | > | | | Strategies for memory improvement |
| Biological psychology: Stress | > | | | |
| Social psychology: Social influence | > | | | |
| Individual differences: Psychotherapy (abnormality) | > | | | |

## KEY TERMS

### Cognitive interview (CI)

- A police technique for interviewing witnesses to a crime.
- Based on what psychologists have found out about memory.
- Because our memory is made up of a network of associations rather than of discrete events, memories are best accessed using multiple retrieval strategies.
- Unlike a standard interview, the CI encourages witnesses to recreate the original context so as to increase the accessibility of stored information.

### Standard interview

- An interview that lacks the four CI components.

## The cognitive interview

### (Fisher and Gieselman, 1992)

1 **Report everything** – Include every single detail of the event, even though it may seem irrelevant. Aims to increase consistency between actual event and recall of event, thus increasing accuracy of recall.
2 **Mental reinstatement of original context** – Mentally recreate the environment from the original incident. Aim is same as for no.1.
3 **Changing the order** – e.g. reversing the order in which events occurred. Aims to vary route through memory in order to increase recall.
4 **Changing the perspective** – Recall the incident from multiple perspectives, e.g. imagining how it would have appeared to other witnesses present at the time. Aim is same as for no.3.

Enhanced CI includes additional techniques for probing witness's mental image of an event.

 Research**EVIDENCE**

**Köhnken et al.** conducted a **meta-analysis** of 53 studies and found a 34% increase in correct recall using CI compared with **standard interview**.

**Milne and Bull** conducted a **lab experiment** using college students and children, where using steps 1 and 2 (report everything and mental reinstatement) gave better recall than when using just one component. They also found that using just one component was no better than an instruction to 'try again'.

**Stein and Memon** tested female cleaning staff in Brazil and found increased recall, especially for details that would be useful e.g. description of man holding the gun.

 Evaluation

**Validity** – Many of the studies tested volunteer witnesses (often college students) in a lab, which may not generalise to everyday life.

**Hard to evaluate** because there are many versions of CI used by different police forces, some just use one or two components and are not comparable to the full version.

**More time-consuming** than standard interview, police officers prefer to use strategies that limit amount of information collected (**Kebbell and Wagstaff**).

**⊂ PUTTING IT ALL TOGETHER**

The cognitive interview is based on psychological insights into memory processes and has proved effective, though the limitations (e.g. too time-consuming) may outweigh the advantages.

| Cognitive psychology: Memory | > | Models of memory | > | Eyewitness testimony |
| Developmental psychology: Early social development | > | Memory in everyday life | > | Cognitive interview |
| Research methods | > | | | Strategies for memory improvement |
| Biological psychology: Stress | > | | | |
| Social psychology: Social influence | > | | | |
| Individual differences: Psychotherapy (abnormality) | > | | | |

## Memory improvement

 ### Verbal techniques

1  **Acronyms** – e.g. ROYGBIV to remember the colours of the rainbow: **R**ed, **O**range, **Y**ellow, **G**reen, **B**lue, **I**ndigo, **V**iolet.
2  **Acrostics** – e.g. **M**y **V**ery **E**asy **M**ethod **J**ust **S**peeds **U**p **N**aming **P**lanets is used to remember the order of the planets: **M**ercury, **V**enus, **E**arth, **M**ars, **J**upiter, **S**aturn, **U**ranus, **N**eptune, **P**luto.
3  **Rhymes** – e.g. using the tune of *Twinkle Twinkle Little Star* to remember the letters of the alphabet.
4  **Chunking** – e.g. telephone numbers and post codes.

 ### ResearchEVIDENCE

**Role of organisation** – **Bower et al.** conducted a **lab experiment**. They gave participants 112 words to learn. Recall was 2–3 times better if the words were presented in an organised hierarchy rather than in a random order. Our memories naturally organise themselves, making links – using mnemonic techniques merely speeds up this process.

**Role of elaborative rehearsal** – **Craik and Tulving** conducted a **lab experiment**. They gave participants words to learn and for each word asked participants one of three questions. (1) Is the word in capital letters? (shallow processing), (2) Does the word rhyme with _____ ? (phonemic processing), (3) A question that analysed meaning e.g. 'Is the word a piece of fruit?' (semantic processing). Words in group 3 were recalled best.

⟳ **PUTTING IT ALL TOGETHER**

Research shows that people who learn about **mnemonic techniques** are better at learning material, so these techniques work. However it is important to select the appropriate technique for the task.

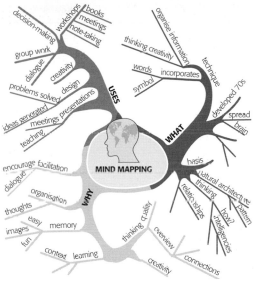

▲ *A mind map about mind mapping*

 ### Visual techniques

1  **Method of loci** – Learner associates material to be learned with different locations in a house, along a road, etc. Then the learner mentally retraces their steps to recall the items.
2  **Keyword method** – Used when associating pieces of information, e.g. learning a new language. The new word is broken into components with images created for each component that link to English meaning.
3  **Mind maps** – Main topic is placed in the centre and then branching links are made producing a unique visual appearance.

 ### ResearchEVIDENCE

**Dual coding hypothesis** – **Pavio** suggested that words and images are processed separately (based on the fact that some brain damaged individuals can process one but not the other). Therefore, concrete words will be remembered better because they are double-encoded – once as a word, and once as a visual image.

**Bower** conducted a **lab experiment**. He found that participants who were asked to mentally produce an image linking a pair of words (e.g. cat and brick) could recall 80% of the words when given cued recall (given first word of pair and asked for second word), whereas 'non-imagers' recalled only 45%. Shows the value of double-encoding.

# Chapter 2

# Developmental psychology

*Column 1: tick when you have produced brief notes.*

*Column 2: tick when you have a good grasp of this topic.*

*Column 3: tick during the final revision when you feel you have complete mastery of the topic.*

| Key terms<br>• **3 marks worth of material** | 1 | 2 | 3 |
|---|---|---|---|
| Attachment | | | |
| Secure attachment | | | |
| Insecure attachment | | | |
| Disruption of attachment | | | |
| Privation | | | |
| Institutionalisation | | | |
| Day care | | | |
| **Research studies related to …**<br>• **6 marks worth of description**<br>• **6 marks worth of evaluation (including the issues of reliability, validity and ethics)** | | | |
| Learning theory explanation of attachment | | | |
| Bowlby's theory of attachment | | | |
| Types of attachment | | | |
| Ainsworth's studies | | | |
| Cultural variations in attachment | | | |
| Disruption of attachment | | | |
| Failure to form attachment (privation) | | | |
| Effects of institutionalisation | | | |
| Impact of day care on social development | | | |
| Impact of day care on aggression | | | |
| Impact of day care on peer relations | | | |
| **Factors that affect …**<br>• **6 marks worth of material** | | | |
| Types of attachment | | | |
| Effects of disruption of attachment | | | |
| Effects of privation | | | |
| Effects of institutionalisation | | | |
| Impact of day care on social development | | | |
| Impact of day care on aggression | | | |
| Impact of day care on peer relations | | | |
| **Explanations/theories**<br>• **6 marks worth of description**<br>• **6 marks worth of evaluation (both strengths and weaknesses)** | | | |
| Learning theory | | | |
| Bowlby's theory (evolutionary perspective) | | | |
| **Applications of attachment research**<br>• **6 marks worth of material** | | | |
| Implications of attachment research | | | |
| Implications of day care research | | | |

## KEY TERMS

### Attachment
- An emotional bond between two people.
- A two-way process that endures over time.
- Leads to certain behaviours such as clinging and proximity-seeking.
- Serves the function of protecting an infant.

### Classical conditioning
- A new response (**conditioned response, CR**) is learned when a **neutral stimulus (NS)** is associated with an **unconditioned stimulus (UCS)**. Initially, the UCS produced an **unconditioned response (UCR)**. After learning, the NS becomes a **conditioned stimulus (CS)** which produces a CR.
- 'Unconditioned' means learning was not required.

### Learning theory
- The name given to a group of explanations i.e. classical and operant conditioning.
- Essentially, these explain behaviour in terms of learning rather than any inborn tendencies (the biological/evolutionary approach) or higher order thinking (the cognitive approach).

### Operant conditioning
- Each time you do something and it results in a *pleasant consequence*, the behaviour is 'stamped in' (**reinforcement**). It becomes more probable that you will repeat that behaviour in the future.
- If you do something and it results in an *unpleasant consequence* (**punishment**), it becomes less likely that you will repeat that behaviour.
- A **reinforcer** is anything that provides reinforcement. A **primary reinforcer** is an innate reinforcer. A **secondary reinforcer** is one that is acquired through experience.

## Learning theory

### Classical conditioning – learning through association
*Before conditioning*
- Unconditioned stimulus (**UCS**) produces unconditioned response (**UCR**).
- Food (**UCS**) produces a sense of pleasure (**UCR**).

*During conditioning*
- Food (**UCS**) and the presence of a person who feeds the infant (**NS**) occur together a number of times. The NS gradually becomes a conditioned stimulus (**CS**).

*After conditioning*
- Conditioned stimulus (**CS**) produces a conditioned response (**CR**).
- Person who feeds the infant (**CS**) produces pleasure (now a **CR**).

### Operant conditioning – learning through reinforcement
- Dollard and Miller suggested that attachment is based on **reinforcement**.
- Hungry infant feels uncomfortable, creating a drive to reduce discomfort.
- When the infant is fed, the drive is reduced and this produces a feeling of pleasure (which is reinforcing). Food becomes a **primary reinforcer**.
- The person who supplies the food is associated with avoiding discomfort and becomes a **secondary reinforcer**, a source of reward.
- Attachment occurs because the infant seeks the person who can supply the reward.

 Evaluation

### Strength
**Learning theory is correct** because we do learn through association and reinforcement – but not because food is the reinforcer; attention and responsiveness certainly reinforce infants behaviours.

### Limitation
**Feeding is not the key criterion**. Infants are more likely to become attached to the person who offers contact comfort rather than the person who feeds them.
- **Harlow** conducted an **animal experiment**. Infant rhesus monkeys were placed in a cage with two wire mothers. The 'lactating mother' had a feeding bottle attached, and the other was wrapped in soft cloth but offered no food. The monkeys spent most time with the cloth-covered mother and would cling to it, especially when they were frightened (a proximity-seeking behaviour which is characteristic of attachment).
- **Schaffer and Emerson** conducted a **controlled observation** of 60 babies in their own homes for a period of about a year. They found that in fact infants were *not* most attached to the person who fed them.

### PUTTING IT ALL TOGETHER

'Cupboard love' is not likely to be the best explanation for attachment because research shows that infants do not necessarily become most strongly attached to the person who feeds them. However, classical and operant conditioning may be part of the story of attachment because attention and responsiveness can be reinforcing.

11

## KEY TERMS

### Continuity hypothesis
- The view that there is a link between an infant's early attachment relationship and later behaviour.

### Internal working model
- A cluster of concepts about relationships.
- In the short-term, it gives the child insight into the caregiver's behaviour.
- In the long-term, it acts as a template for future relationships because it generates expectations about how people behave.

### Monotropy
- The idea that the one relationship that the infant has with his/her primary attachment figure is of special significance in emotional development.

### Primary attachment figure
- The person who has formed the closest bond with a child.
- Demonstrated by the intensity of the relationship.
- Usually a child's biological mother, but could be an adoptive mother, a father, grandmother, etc.

### Secondary attachment figure
- Acts as a kind of emotional safety net.
- Contributes to social development.

### Sensitive period
- A biologically-determined period of time during which a child is particularly sensitive to a specific form of stimulation.
- Resulting in the development of a specific response or characteristic.

### Social releasers
- A social behaviour or characteristic which elicits a caregiving reaction.

### Temperament hypothesis
- The view that attachment type can be explained in terms of an infant's innate temperament rather than caregiver sensitivity.

## The evolutionary perspective (Bowlby, 1969)

- Babies have an innate drive to become attached and also are born with certain characteristics, called **social releasers**, which elicit caregiving.
- Attachment develops during a **sensitive period**, around 3–6 months. Later, it becomes increasingly difficult to form attachments.
- Infants have one special emotional bond (**monotropy**) with their **primary attachment figure**.
- Infants have many **secondary attachments** that are important for healthy psychological and social development.
- The mother–infant relationship creates expectations about relationships, leading to an **internal working model**.
- The **continuity hypothesis** is that individuals who are securely attached in infancy *continue* to be socially and emotionally competent.

 Research**EVIDENCE** supporting Bowlby's theory

**Universality** – If attachment is an innate process, it should follow the same pattern in all cultures. **Tronick et al.** conducted a **cross-cultural study** of the Efe, an African tribe from Zaire, whose infants are looked after, and even breastfed, by different women. Despite such different childrearing practices, the infants still showed one primary attachment at 6 months.

**Monotropy** – **Schaffer and Emerson**'s **controlled observation** found that infants formed many attachments, but there was still one *primary* object of attachment which most often (but not always) was the infant's mother.

**Caregiver sensitivity** – **Harlow**'s study showed that monkeys raised with an unresponsive wire 'mother' developed into maladjusted adults.

**Continuity hypothesis** – A **longitudinal study** by **Sroufe et al.** (Minnesota longitudinal study) found that infants classified as secure were later rated highest for social competence and popularity.

 Evaluation

### Strengths
1 **Makes sense that behaviours would have evolved to ensure safety** of offspring and attachment is, therefore, an innate predisposition.
2 **Research support** for key concepts such as sensitivity and continuity, for example Ainsworth's research.

### Limitations
1 **Monotropy**. Not clear whether only one primary attachment is necessary for healthy emotional development; it may be better to have several.
2 **Alternative explanation**, the **temperament hypothesis** – **Kagan** suggested that attachment could be explained in terms of innate temperamental types. Infants who have an 'easy' temperament are more likely to become securely attached and those who are 'difficult' tend to be insecurely attached.

###  PUTTING IT ALL TOGETHER

Bowlby's evolutionary approach to understanding attachment as an adaptive behaviour for both infant and parent continues to be the preferred central explanation for attachment behaviour.

| Cognitive psychology: Memory | > | Attachment | > | Learning theory |
|---|---|---|---|---|
| Developmental psychology: Early social development | > | Attachment in everyday life | > | Bowlby's evolutionary theory |
| Research methods | > | | | **Types of attachment** |
| Biological psychology: Stress | > | | | Cultural variations in attachment |
| Social psychology: Social influence | > | | | Disruption of attachment |
| Individual differences: Psychotherapy (abnormality) | > | | | Failure to form attachment |

## KEY TERMS

### Insecure attachment

- Develops as a result of caregiver's lack of sensitive responding to an infant's needs.
- May be associated with poor cognitive and emotional development.
- **Insecure-avoidant** infants are willing to explore and unresponsive to mother's return; they generally avoid social interaction and intimacy with others.
- **Insecure-resistant (ambivalent)** infants who are less interested in exploring and show distress on mother's return; generally they both seek and reject intimacy and social interaction.
- **Insecure-disorganised** infants who lack consistent patterns of attachment behaviour.
- **Disinhibited** infants who display affection to strangers and may be attention-seeking.

### Secure attachment

- Willing to explore, easy to soothe, high stranger anxiety.
- Infant is comfortable with social interaction and intimacy.
- Related to healthy subsequent cognitive and emotional development.
- Develops as a result of sensitive responding by caregiver to the infant's needs.

### Separation anxiety

- Distress shown by an infant when separated from his/her attachment figure.

### Strange situation

- Method to assess strength of attachment.
- Conducted in a novel environment.
- Involves eight episodes.
- Infant's behaviour observed as mother leaves and returns, and when a stranger is present.
- Measures attachment in terms of stranger anxiety and separation anxiety.

### Stranger anxiety.

- Distress shown by an infant when approached by an unfamiliar person.

# Secure and insecure attachment

 key**STUDIES** Ainsworth

### Ainsworth (1967)

**How?** Method – **naturalistic observation** of 26 infants and their mothers in Uganda.

**Showed?** The mothers who were more sensitive to their infants' needs had more securely attached infants (they cried less and explored more). These results couldn't be explained by **learning theory** but can be explained within Bowlby's theory, related to caregiver sensitivity.

### Ainsworth et al. (1971)

**How?** Method – **naturalistic observation** of 26 infants and their mothers in Baltimore, USA.

**Showed?** Caregiver sensitivity increased attachment, e.g. responsiveness to crying led to secure attachment and decreased crying; contrary to predictions of learning theory.

### Ainsworth et al. (1978)

**How?** Method – **controlled lab observation**, the **strange situation** was used to study 106 middle-class US infants.

**Showed?** Distinct behaviour patterns identified: 66% of infants displayed **secure attachment**, 22% were **insecure-avoidant** and 12% were **insecure-resistant**.

 Research**EVIDENCE**

**Disorganised attachment – Main and Solomon** analysed videotapes of children in the strange situation and identified a fourth attachment type: infants would show very strong attachment behaviour one minute, followed by avoidance or looking fearful towards their caregiver.

**Disinhibited attachment** – A more recently identified type resulting from lack of early attachment. Infants try to form attachments with anyone they meet, but such attachments are superficial.

 Evaluation

**Validity – what is being measured?** The strange situation only measures the attachment within one relationship rather than a quality lodged in the individual. Attachment type may be a sum of many different attachment relationships. However **Main and Weston** found that attachment type is mainly influenced by the mother, i.e. one relationship may determine overall attachment type.

**Predictive validity** – We would expect securely attached infants to have better emotional and social development. This is supported by **Sroufe et al.** (see facing page) and **Hazan and Shaver** who found that people classified as securely attached in early life, later were more trusting.

### PUTTING IT ALL TOGETHER

The concepts of secure and insecure attachment have led to useful insights into infant and adult behaviour, and provide an understanding of how parenting practices can be improved.

| Cognitive psychology: Memory | > | **Attachment** | > | Learning theory |
|---|---|---|---|---|
| **Developmental psychology: Early social development** > | | Attachment in everyday life | > | Bowlby's evolutionary theory |
| Research methods | > | | | Types of attachment |
| Biological psychology: Stress | > | | | **Cultural variations in attachment** |
| Social psychology: Social influence | > | | | Disruption of attachment |
| Individual differences: Psychotherapy (abnormality) | > | | | Failure to form attachment |

## KEY TERMS

### Collectivist culture
- The rules, customs, morals and ways of interacting that bind together members of a society or collection of people.

### Culture
- Any culture that places more value on the 'collective' rather than the individual.
- And on interdependence rather than independence.
- The opposite is true of **individualist culture**.

### Imposed etic
- A technique or theory that is developed in one culture and then used to study the behaviour of people in a different culture.
- Such a technique or theory may be meaningless when used with people who have had different experiences or have different values.

## Cross-cultural similarities

If **attachment** processes are innate (as Bowlby suggested), we would expect to find similarities (called 'universals') across cultures.

###  ResearchEVIDENCE

**Ainsworth**'s studies (see page 13) found various universals in attachment behaviour, e.g. mothers of **securely attached** infants showed greater sensitivity towards their infants than those who were **insecurely attached**.

**Tronick et al.** observed members of the Efe, from Zaire (see page 12). Despite using childrearing practices that are quite different from those in Western **individualist** cultures, the infants still showed one **primary attachment** at 6 months.

**Fox** observed infants raised on Israeli kibbutzim in communal children's homes. Infants showed greater attachment to their mothers despite spending more time with the *metapelet* (community nurses), presumably because their mothers showed greater sensitivity.

**Van IJzendoorn and Kroonenberg** conducted a **meta-analysis** of 32 studies. Variations within cultures was 1.5 times greater than between cultures, suggesting that cultural practices have little influence on attachment behaviour.

## Cross-cultural differences

If cultural differences in attachment are observed, this suggests that culturally-determined childrearing practices (rather than inherited processes) affect attachment.

###  ResearchEVIDENCE

**Grossmann and Grossmann** found that German infants tended to be classified as insecurely, rather than securely, attached.

**Takahashi** found that Japanese infants showed much higher rates of **insecure-resistant attachment** (32%) than most other cultures, and no evidence of **insecure-avoidant attachment**.

###  Overall evaluation

**Culture bias – Rothbaum et al.** argued that attachment theory has a strong Western bias, reflecting individualist ideas of the importance of autonomy. In collectivist societies, such as Japan, carers' sensitivity leads to dependence, inhibition of emotional expression and less desire to explore.

**Culture and country** – Within any country there are many cultures, yet most research refers to countries such as Japan or America. Such research may lack **validity** because many different cultural practices have been lumped together.

**Cross-cultural research** involves the use of **imposed etics** making the findings meaningless. For example:
- Japanese infants are rarely separated from their mothers so their apparent distress on separation is not because of insecure attachment, but because they are never separated.
- German infants may appear to be insecurely attached but this is because German culture discourages closeness, so infants would be less likely to show proximity-seeking behaviours in the **strange situation**.

## C PUTTING IT ALL TOGETHER

**Prior and Glaser** conclude that expressions of maternal sensitivity and manifestations of secure-base behaviour may vary across cultures, but the core concepts are universal.

| Cognitive psychology: Memory | > | Attachment | > | Learning theory |
| Developmental psychology: Early social development | > | Attachment in everyday life | > | Bowlby's evolutionary theory |
| Research methods | > | | | Types of attachment |
| Biological psychology: Stress | > | | | Cultural variations in attachment |
| Social psychology: Social influence | > | | | Disruption of attachment |
| Individual differences: Psychotherapy (abnormality) | > | | | Failure to form attachment |

## KEY TERMS

### Institutional care

- An 'institution' is a place dedicated to a particular task, such as looking after children awaiting adoption, caring for the mentally ill, or looking after patients in hospital.
- A place where people are looked after for a period of time, as opposed to **day care** or outpatient care where people go home every day.
- In the past, such institutions had fairly strict regimes and offered little emotional care.

 Individual**DIFFERENCES**

There is an interaction between security of attachment and the effects of attachment disruption – children who are **securely attached** appear to cope better with disruption.

**Bowlby et al.** studied children who were in institutional care (a TB sanatorium) when young. Some of the children were later quite normal, whereas others were maladjusted – Bowlby et al. suggested that those who coped better may have been securely attached.

## Disruption of attachment

Bowlby's theory predicted that disruption of **attachment** in early life is likely to have a negative effect on social and emotional development.

###  key**STUDY** Robertson and Robertson (1963–1973)

**How?** Method – **naturalistic observations** recorded in films. Six children (aged less than 3) were studied during periods of brief separation from their **primary attachment figure**: Laura was in hospital; John was in a residential nursery; and Jane, Lucy, Thomas and Kate were looked after by the Robinsons in their home where they received a high level of substitute emotional care.

**Showed?** Laura and John became depressed and withdrawn. The other children coped well and returned to their families happily. *Physical* separation, as in the cases of Jane, Lucy, Thomas and Kate, did not have a negative outcome because substitute emotional care was offered. In contrast, the *emotional* disruption experienced by Laura and John did appear to have negative consequences.

**Validity?** These were **case studies** of unique individuals and situations, which means they may lack generalisability. However, the data collected was rich in detail.

### Research**EVIDENCE**

**Spitz and Wolf** observed that 100 'normal' children in **institutional care** became severely depressed within a few months of being placed there.

**Skeels and Dye** suggested that lack of emotional care may harm intellectual development. This was based on a case where a group of institutionalised children with low IQs later improved after they were transferred to a home for mentally retarded adults (substitute emotional care). This was then tested by **Skodak and Skeels**. One group of infants in institutional care was transferred to a home for mentally retarded adults, while a control group remained in the orphanage. After 1.5 years the IQs of the control group had fallen whereas the transferred group's IQs had risen from 64 to 92 points.

**Bohman and Sigvardsson** studied over 600 adopted children in Sweden. At the age of 11, 26% of them were classified as 'problem children'. Ten years later, after successful adoptions, they were the same as 'normal' children in terms of social and emotional development.

**Bifulco et al.** studied 249 women who had lost mothers through separation or death before they were 17. This group was twice as likely to suffer from **depressive** or **anxiety** disorders when the children became adults. This suggests that early disruptions in attachment may make an individual psychologically more vulnerable and, if triggered by stressful events later in life, mental disorders may develop.

### PUTTING IT ALL TOGETHER

The research shows a clear difference between physical and emotional disruption. When children experience physical separation from their primary attachment figure, the resulting disruption of attachment does not have negative effects *as long as* alternative emotional care is provided. However, such children may be more vulnerable in later life when having to cope with stressful situations.

| Cognitive psychology: Memory | > | Attachment | > | Learning theory |
| Developmental psychology: Early social development | > | Attachment in everyday life | > | Bowlby's evolutionary theory |
| Research methods | > | | | Types of attachment |
| Biological psychology: Stress | > | | | Cultural variations in attachment |
| Social psychology: Social influence | > | | | Disruption of attachment |
| Individual differences: Psychotherapy (abnormality) | > | | | **Failure to form attachment** |

## KEY TERMS

### Attachment disorder

- A psychiatric disorder characterised by an individual's inability to identify a preferred **attachment** figure.
- Individuals typically show an inability to interact and relate to others, evident before the age of 5.
- Individuals may lack a conscience and be unable to trust others or form lasting relationships.

### Deprivation dwarfism

- Children who experience emotional deprivation are often physically smaller.
- Emotional disturbance (stress) may affect the production of **hormones**, such as growth hormones, and lead to a kind of 'dwarfism'.

### Privation

- The failure to develop any attachments during early life.
- This is contrasted with 'deprivation' or 'disruption' where attachment bonds have formed, but may be disrupted. Such disruption may last for weeks or a lifetime (in the case of parental death).

# Failure to form attachment

 Research**EVIDENCE**

**Isolated children** – Method – **case studies**.

1  **Genie** was locked in a room by her father until she was 13½ (because he thought she was retarded). She never fully recovered socially and lacked social responsiveness. Her lack of recovery may be due to her extreme early emotional **privation** (though she may have been attached to her mother), or due to being retarded, or because she was beyond the **sensitive period** for attachment when discovered, or because of the physical deprivation she experienced (**Rymer**).

2  The **Czech twins** spent the first seven years of their lives locked up by a stepmother and were unable to talk. They were then well cared for by two loving sisters and, by age 14, had near-normal intellectual and social functioning. By the age of 20, they were of above average intelligence and had excellent relationships with members of their foster family (**Koluchová**).

**Institutional care** – **Hodges and Tizard** conducted a **longitudinal natural experiment**, following a group of children placed in care at less than 4 months old. At age 16, the children who had been adopted were **securely attached** to their families, which was not true of the children who had returned to their natural families. However, both groups of ex-institutional children had problems with peers (e.g. were less likely to have a best friend) and sought more attention from adults (a sign of **disinhibited attachment**).

**Romanian orphans** – **Rutter et al.** conducted a **longitudinal study** of a group of about 100 Romanian orphans adopted by UK families. The children who were adopted by British families before the age of 6 months showed 'normal' emotional development. However, many of the Romanian orphans adopted after 6 months showed **disinhibited attachments** and had problems with peers.

 Effects of failure to form attachment (privation)

**Attachment disorder** is likely to be caused by the experience of severe neglect or frequent change of caregivers in early life. Individuals with attachment disorder may be *reactive/inhibited* (withdrawn, unable to cope with most social situations) or *disinhibited* (overfriendly and attention-seeking).

**Poor parenting** – **Quinton et al.** found that ex-institutional women often had difficulties as parents, creating a cycle of privation. More of the ex-institutional women were rated as lacking in warmth when interacting with their children and had children who have spent time in care.

**Deprivation dwarfism** – **Gardner** recorded **case studies**, such as one girl who, from birth, had to be fed through a tube. Her mother never cuddled the girl, in fear of dislodging the tube. By 8 months old, the child was severely withdrawn and physically stunted. When admitted to hospital, she was given lots of attention and soon returned to normal, despite no change in her diet.

↻ **PUTTING IT ALL TOGETHER**

This research suggests that children who *lack* early attachments are likely to experience permanent emotional and social difficulties later in life, though these effects may be less severe if subsequent emotional care is given.

| Cognitive psychology: Memory | > | Attachment | > | The impact of day care |
| Developmental psychology: Early social development | > | Attachment in everyday life | > | Implications for child care practices |
| Research methods | > | | | |
| Biological psychology: Stress | > | | | |
| Social psychology: Social influence | > | | | |
| Individual differences: Psychotherapy (abnormality) | > | | | |

# The impact of day care on social development

 Negative effects

**Violata and Russell** conducted a **meta-analysis** of 88 studies and concluded that day care for more than 20 hours per week had an unmistakably negative effect on socio-emotional development, behaviour and **attachment** of young children.

 Positive effects

**Clarke-Stewart et al.** studied 150 children and found that those who were in day care were consistently more advanced in their social development than children who stayed home with mothers. These advances were in social development, independence, dinnertime obedience, compliance requests and social interactions with peers.

**Sylva et al.** studied the development of 3000 children in various preschool educational settings. This study found increased independence and sociability in children who attended day care.

 Weaknesses of research

Research does not demonstrate that day care has *caused* any later behaviours – only **correlations** have been demonstrated. **Dingfelder** suggests that we need to better understand the processes, e.g. what particular elements of day care may lead to negative outcomes?

## KEY TERMS

**Day care**
- A form of temporary care (i.e. not all day and night).
- Not provided by parents.
- Usually takes place outside the home.

 Mediating factors

- **Quality of care** – low quality care associated with poor social development (**NICHD**)
- **Individual differences** – shy children may find day care more difficult (**Pennebaker et al.**).
- **Child's age** – Children who start day care before 18 months are more likely to experience negative effects (**Gregg et al.**).
- **Number of hours** Children who attend day care full-time may be worse off.

## Impact of day care on aggressiveness

 Negative effects

The **NICHD** study is a **longitudinal study** conducted the US since 1991, involving over 1000 children from diverse families and locations. At age 5, children who had been in day care of any kind were rated as more assertive, disobedient and aggressive. Children in full-time day care (more than 30 hours) were about three times more likely to show behaviour problems (e.g. arguing, temper tantrums, lying and hitting) compared with those cared for by their mothers at home.

The **EPPE study** found similar results in UK samples. High levels of day care, particularly nursery care in the first 2 years, may elevate the risk of developing anti-social behaviour (**Sammons et al.**).

 Weaknesses of research

The **NICHD** study results can also be used to show that day care is *not* necessarily associated with aggressiveness; 83% of children attending **day care** for less than 30 hours per week did *not* show higher levels of aggression (**Friedman**). This underlies the importance of looking carefully at the findings.

**NICHD** data also showed that a mother's sensitivity to her child was a better indicator of reported problem behaviours than was time in child care (less sensitivity = more problem behaviours).

## Impact of day care on peer relations

 Negative effects

**Belsky and Rovine** found that children who had received 20 hours or more of day care per week before they were 1 year old were more likely to be **insecurely attached** compared with children at home.

 Positive effects

Day care exposes children to their peers and thus permits them time to develop social strategies, such as the ability to negotiate and make friends.

**Field** conducted a **correlational study** and found that the amount of time spent in full-time day care was **positively correlated** to the number of friends a child had once they went to school.

**Clarke-Stewart et al.** found that those children who attended day care were more able to deal with peer relationships, e.g. being better at settling disputes.

 **PUTTING IT ALL TOGETHER**

There is evidence for both positive and negative effects of day care, or no effects at all. A child's development is influenced by an array of different factors, only one of which is day care.

| Cognitive psychology: Memory | > | Attachment | > | The impact of day care | |
|---|---|---|---|---|---|
| **Developmental psychology: Early social development** | > | **Attachment in everyday life** | > | **Implications for child care practices** | |
| Research methods | > | | | | |
| Biological psychology: Stress | > | | | | |
| Social psychology: Social influence | > | | | | |
| Individual differences: Psychotherapy (abnormality) | > | | | | |

## Implications of attachment research

The findings of **attachment** research has implications for:

**Institutional care** (such as hospitals and adoption centres) – The research by **Robertson and Robertson** (see page 15) demonstrated the importance of high quality emotional care in such settings.

**Adoption** – **Bowlby's** theory identified the importance of early experiences for later emotional and social development, further demonstrated by **Hodges and Tizard** and **Rutter et al.** (see page 16). This is important for arranging adoptions of children because late adoptions (after 6 months) may have negative effects. Today, most babies are adopted within the first week of birth and research shows that adoptive mothers and children are just as securely attached as non-adoptive families (**Singer et al.**).

**Parenting practices** – Parents who had poor attachment experiences themselves may need assistance to learn parenting skills (see **Quinton et al.** page 16).

**Day care practises** – The potential negative effects may be countered by recognising the role of day care workers as attachment figures. The Soho Family Centre in London bases its day care programme on attachment theory. Each carer is assigned a maximum of three children and is paired with another carer who can step in if need be.

## Implications of day care research

The findings of **day care** research has implications about:

**High quality day care** – This is associated with positive outcomes, whereas negative effects may be due to low-quality care.

Psychologists have identified the following key characteristics of quality day care:

- **Low child-to-staff ratios** – The **NICHD** study found that it day care staff could only provide sensitive care if the ratios were as low as 3:1.

- **Minimal staff turnover** – When staff come and go, children may either fail to form attachments to them or, if they have formed an attachment, they suffer the anxiety associated with disruption of attachment when the staff go (**Schaffer**).

- **Sensitive emotional care** – The **NICHD** study found that about 23% of infant care providers give 'highly' sensitive infant care whereas 20% are 'emotionally detached' from the infants under their care.

- **Qualified and experienced staff** – **Sylva et al.** found that quality was associated with the qualification levels of the day care staff.

The quality of day care in the UK is monitored by Ofsted (who inspect schools as well) to insure high quality care.

It is also promoted and monitored in the UK by the SureStart programme and the associated NESS project (National Evaluation of SureStart, **Melhuish et al.**).

"IT WAS A GREAT IDEA to OPEN A DAY CARE CENTER FOR KIDS WHOSE PARENTS ARE HUNTING AND GATHERING."

## ⟳ PUTTING IT ALL TOGETHER

It is clear that psychological research into attachment and day care has had, and continues to have, an important effect on the way we look after children both in their own homes and when they need to be cared for outside the home.

# Chapter 3

# Research methods

*Column 1: tick when you have produced brief notes.*

*Column 2: tick when you have a good grasp of this topic.*

*Column 3: tick during the final revision when you feel you have complete mastery of the topic.*

| Key terms/concepts<br>• **What, how and why (advantages and weaknesses)** | 1 | 2 | 3 |
|---|---|---|---|
| Experimental method<br>• Laboratory, field, natural<br>• Experimental design (independent groups, repeated measures, and matched pairs)<br>• Advantages and weaknesses | | | |
| Studies using a correlational analysis<br>• Analysis and interpretation of correlational data<br>• Positive and negative correlations<br>• Interpretation of correlation coefficients.<br>• Advantages and weaknesses | | | |
| Observational techniques<br>• Design of naturalistic observations<br>• Development and use of behavioural categories<br>• Advantages and weaknesses | | | |
| Self-report techniques<br>• Design of questionnaires and interviews<br>• Advantages and weaknesses | | | |
| Case studies<br>• Advantages and weaknesses | | | |
| Validity<br>• Control of extraneous variables<br>• Demand characteristics and Investigator effects<br>• How to deal with low validity | | | |
| Reliability<br>• How to deal with low reliability | | | |
| Ethical issues<br>• Ways in which psychologists deal with them<br>• Awareness of the BPS Code of Ethics | | | |
| Selection of participants<br>• Sampling techniques including random, opportunity and volunteer sampling. | | | |
| Aims and hypotheses<br>• Including directional and non directional | | | |
| Operationalisation of variables<br>• Including independent and dependant variables | | | |
| Pilot studies | | | |
| Quantitative data, presentation and interpretation<br>• Graphs, scattergrams and tables.<br>• Measures of central tendency including median, mean, mode<br>• Measures of dispersion including ranges and standard deviation | | | |
| Qualitative data, analysis and presentation<br>• Processes involved in content analysis | | | |

| Cognitive psychology: Memory | | Methods and techniques > | Advantages and weaknesses |
| Developmental psychology: Early social development > | Investigation design > | |
| **Research methods** > | Data analysis | |
| Biological psychology: Stress > | and presentation > | |
| Social psychology: Social influence > | | |
| Individual differences: Psychotherapy (abnormality) > | | |

| Method/technique | | Nature and use | Advantages and weaknesses |
|---|---|---|---|
| **Experiments** | **Lab experiment** | **IV** manipulated to observe effect on **DV**, highly controlled. | + Can draw causal conclusion.<br>+ **Extraneous variables** minimised.<br>+ Can be easily replicated.<br>– Contrived, tends to lack **mundane realism**.<br>– **Investigator** and **participant effects**. |
| | **Field experiment** | More natural surroundings, IV directly manipulated by experimenter to observe effect on DV, some control. | + Can draw causal conclusion.<br>+ Usually higher **ecological validity**.<br>+ Avoids some **participant effects**.<br>– Less control.<br>– May have **demand characteristics**. |
| | **Natural experiment** | IV not directly manipulated, participants not randomly allocated. | + Allows research where the IV can't be manipulated for ethical/practical reasons.<br>+ Enables psychologists to study 'real' problems.<br>– Cannot demonstrate causal relationships.<br>– Inevitably many **extraneous variables**.<br>– **Investigator** and **participant effects**. |
| **Studies using a correlational analysis** | | **Co-variables** examined for positive, negative or zero association. | + Can be used when not possible to manipulate variables.<br>+ Can rule out a causal relationship.<br>– People often misinterpret correlations.<br>– There may be other, unknown variables. |
| **Observational techniques** | **Naturalistic observation** | Everything left as normal, all variables free to vary. | + Study behaviour where can't manipulate variables.<br>+ High **ecological validity**.<br>– Poor control of **extraneous variables**.<br>– **Observer bias**, low **inter-observer reliability**. |
| | **Controlled observation** | Some variables controlled by researcher, e.g. the environment. | + Can manipulate variables to observe effects.<br>– Less natural, reduced **ecological validity**.<br>– **Investigator** and **participant effects**.<br>– **Observer bias**, low **inter-observer reliability**. |
| | **Content analysis** | Indirect observation of behaviour based on written or verbal material such as interviews or TV. | + High **ecological validity** because based on what people do.<br>+ Can be replicated easily because sources are publicly available.<br>– **Observer bias**. |
| **Self-report techniques** | **Questionnaires** | Set of written questions. | + Can be easily repeated, so lots of people can be questioned.<br>+ Respondents may be more willing to reveal personal information.<br>+ Does not require specialist administrators.<br>– **Leading questions, social desirability bias**.<br>– Biased samples. |
| | **Interviews** | **Unstructured interviews** where the interviewer develops questions in response to respondent's answers, conducted in real time. | + More detailed information collected.<br>+ Can access unexpected information.<br>– **Social desirability bias, interviewer bias, inter-interviewer reliability, leading questions**.<br>– Requires well-trained personnel. |
| **Case studies** | | Detailed study of a single individual, institution or event. Involves many different techniques, e.g. interviews, psychological tests. | + Rich, in-depth data collected.<br>+ Used to investigate unusual instances of behaviour.<br>+ Complex interactions studied.<br>– Lacks generalisability.<br>– May involve unreliable, retrospective recall.<br>– Researcher may lack objectivity. |

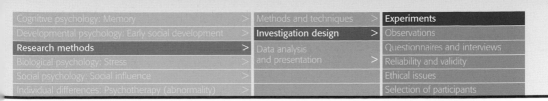

| | | | Experiments |
|---|---|---|---|
| Cognitive psychology: Memory | > | Methods and techniques | > |
| Developmental psychology: Early social development | | Investigation design | > | Observations |
| Research methods | > | Data analysis | | Questionnaires and interviews |
| Biological psychology: Stress | > | and presentation | > | Reliability and validity |
| Social psychology: Social influence | > | | | Ethical issues |
| Individual differences: Psychotherapy (abnormality) | > | | | Selection of participants |

## Designing experiments

 ### Independent and dependent variables

**Independent variable (IV)** is an event that is directly manipulated by the experimenter in order to observe its effects on the DV.

**Dependent variable (DV)** depends in some way on the IV.

Variables must be **operationalised**, i.e. defined in a way that they can be tested. For example, instead of a DV 'educational attainment', an experimenter must specify a way to measure this, such as GCSE grades.

 ### Aims and hypotheses

The **aim** of any study is a statement of what the researcher intends to investigate. A **hypothesis** is a precise and testable statement about the expected relationship between variables.

A hypothesis may be **directional** where it states the direction of the predicted difference or relationship between two conditions or two groups of participants. Or it may be **non-directional**, simply predicting that there will be a difference or relationship between two conditions or two groups of participants, without stating the direction.

### Experimental design

A set of procedures used to control the influence of factors such as **participant variables** in an experiment.

**Repeated measures**

| Same participants in every condition being tested | + Good control for **participant variables**.<br>+ Fewer participants needed.<br>– **Order effects** (e.g. boredom, practice).<br>– Participants may guess the purpose of the experiment. |
|---|---|

**Independent groups**

| Participants are allocated to two (or more) groups representing different experimental conditions. | + Avoids **order effects** and participants guessing the purpose of the experiment.<br>– Needs more participants.<br>– No control of **participant variables** (can use **random allocation**). |
|---|---|

**Matched pairs**

| Pairs of participants matched on key **participant variables**. One member of each pair is placed in the experimental group and the other member in the control group. | + Avoids **order effects**.<br>+ **Participant variables** partly controlled.<br>– Matching is difficult and never totally successful. |
|---|---|

**Counterbalancing** can be used to deal with order effects by ensuring that each condition is tested first or second in equal amounts.
- Some participants receive condition A then B, others received B then A.
- Or ABBA – All participants receive A B then B A.

### Groups and conditions

In an experiment using a **repeated measures** or **matched pairs design** each participant takes part in two or more conditions. The **experimental condition** (or conditions) contains the independent variable. The **control condition** provides a baseline measure of behaviour without the experimental treatment (IV), so that the effect of the experimental treatment may be assessed. In an experiment using an **independent groups design**, there is an **experimental group** and a **control group.**

**Demand characteristics**
- A cue that makes participants aware of what the researcher expects to find or how participants are expected to behave.

**Extraneous variable (EV)**
- Any variable, other than the IV, which may potentially affect the DV and thereby confound the findings.
- Order effects, participant variables and situational variables may act as EVs.

**Order effects**
- In a repeated measures design, an extraneous variable arising from the order in which conditions are presented.
- For example, participants do better the second time because they have had practice (practice effect).

**Random allocation**
- Allocating participants to experimental groups using random techniques.

 ### Control of variables

'Control' refers to the extent to which any variable is held constant or regulated by a researcher. The IV is controlled to observe its effect. EVs are controlled so any effect can be attributed to the IV, for example:

- **Participant variables** such as age, intelligence, motivation, etc. may explain why participants in one group do better.

- **Situational variables** such as time of day, temperature, noise, etc. may also explain group differences.

- **Investigator effects**, where an investigator unwittingly communicates information.

- **Demand characteristics** trigger a predictable response.

Methods of control include:
- **Single blind technique** – Participants don't know the true aims of a study.

- **Double blind technique** – Investigators and participants don't know the true aims of a study.

| Cognitive psychology: Memory | > | Methods and techniques | > | Experiments |
| Developmental psychology: Early social development | > | **Investigation design** | > | **Observations** |
| **Research methods** | > | Data analysis and presentation | | **Questionnaires and interviews** |
| Biological psychology: Stress | > | | > | Reliability and validity |
| Social psychology: Social influence | > | | | Ethical issues |
| Individual differences: Psychotherapy (abnormality) | > | | | Selection of participants |

# Observational design

##  Behavioural categories

It is necessary to devise objective methods to separate the continuous stream of action into separate **behavioural categories**, i.e. **operationalise** the target behaviour(s). This can be done using:

- **Behaviour checklist** – A list of component behaviours.
- **Coding system** – Individual behaviours are given a code for ease of recording.

The behavioural categories should:

- Be *objective* – The observer should not have to make inferences about the behaviour.
- Cover *all possible component behaviours* and avoid a 'waste basket' category.
- Be *mutually exclusive*, meaning that you should not have to mark two categories at one time.

##  Sampling procedures

In many situations, continuous observation is not possible because there would be too much data to record, therefore there must be a systematic method of **sampling** observations:

- **Event sampling** – Counting the number of times a certain behaviour (event) occurs in a target individual.
- **Time sampling** – Recording behaviours at regular intervals, e.g. every 30 seconds.

##  Participant and non-participant

In some observations, the observer is also a participant in the behaviour being observed (**participant observation**) which is likely to affect objectivity. More often, the observer is not a participant (**non-participant observation**).

##  Overt and covert

Participants who are aware of being observed (**overt observation**) may alter their behaviour, so **validity** is reduced. Making observations without a participant's knowledge (**covert observations**), such as using one-way mirrors, may raise **ethical issues**.

##  Structured and unstructured

In a **structured observation** the observer uses behavioural categories and sampling procedures to structure the observations. In a **controlled observation** both the observations and the environment are controlled (structured); in a **naturalistic observation** only the observations are structured.

In an **unstructured observation** the observer records all relevant behaviour but has no system.

**KEY TERMS**
**Pilot study**

- A small-scale trial of a study.
- Run to test any aspects of the design, with a view to making improvements.

# Questionnaires and interviews

##  Good questions

A 'good question' should be clear and unambiguous. It should not be biased in a way that might suggest particular answers to the respondent (i.e. a **leading question**).

**Closed questions** have a range of answers from which respondents select one.

- They produce **quantitative data** which is easier to analyse.
- Respondents may be forced to select answers that don't represent their real thoughts or behaviour.

**Open questions** invite respondents to provide their own answers rather than select one of those provided. They tend to produce **qualitative data**.

- Can provide unexpected answers and rich detail, allowing researchers to gain new insights.
- More difficult to summarise answers because there may be such a wide variety of responses. This then makes it difficult to draw conclusions.

##  Good questionnaires/interviews

Questions should be unthreatening and easy to answer. More challenging questions will be answered more truthfully once trust is established.

Filler questions may be used that disguise the true aims of the **questionnaire/interview** so that respondents are more honest.

**Sampling techniques** are important in obtaining a representative sample.

A **pilot study** enables questions to be tested on a small group of people. This means you can refine the questions in response to any difficulties encountered.

##  Structured and unstructured

In a **structured interview** the questions are decided in advance and are the same for all participants.

In an **unstructured interview** the questions are unplanned and usually guided by the respondents' answers.

In a **clinical interview** (semi-structured) the interviewer starts with a few standard questions but further questions develop in response to the answers given.

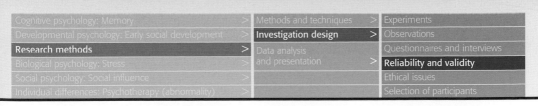

| Cognitive psychology: Memory | > | Methods and techniques | > | Experiments |
| Developmental psychology: Early social development | > | **Investigation design** | > | Observations |
| **Research methods** | > | Data analysis and presentation | > | Questionnaires and interviews |
| Biological psychology: Stress | > | | > | **Reliability and validity** |
| Social psychology: Social influence | > | | | Ethical issues |
| Individual differences: Psychotherapy (abnormality) | > | | | Selection of participants |

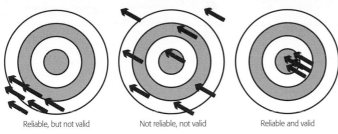

| Reliable, but not valid | Not reliable, not valid | Reliable and valid |

## KEY TERMS

**Reliability**
- A measure of consistency.
- **Internal reliability** concerns consistency *within* a set of scores or items.
- **External reliability** concerns consistency *over time* such that it is possible to obtain the same results on subsequent occasions when the measure is used with the same thing.

**Validity**
- The extent to which a study and its findings are legitimate or true.
- **Internal validity** concerns whether a study has tested what it set out to test.
- **External validity** concerns the degree to which a research finding can be generalised to, for example, other settings (**ecological validity**), or other groups of people (**population validity**) and over time (**historical validity**).
- Any study that has low internal validity must lack generalisability and therefore also has low external validity.

## Reliability

**Experimental studies** The reliability of an experiment can be determined through replication.
- *To improve reliability* **extraneous variables** should be controlled.

**Observational studies – Inter-observer reliability** is the extent to which there is agreement between two or more observers.
- *To assess internal reliability* – Correlate the observations of two or more observers. If (total number of agreements) / (total number of observations) >.80, the data has high inter-observer reliability.
- *To improve reliability* observers trained to use **behavioural categories**.

**Self-report techniques – Inter-interviewer reliability** is the extent to which two interviewers produce the same outcome from an interview.
- *To assess internal reliability* the **split-half method** can be used. Scores/responses on both halves of a test should be the same/consistent.
- *To assess external reliability* the **test-retest method** can be used when the same questionnaire/interview is repeated with the same respondent a few weeks apart.
- *To improve reliability* – remove questions which create inconsistency.

## Validity

**Experimental studies**
- *Internal validity* – The degree to which the observed effect was due to experimental manipulation rather than factors such as **extraneous variables**. It is also affected by **mundane realism** and **experimental realism**.
- *External validity* – The representativeness of the sample affects the ability to generalise the findings to other people and situations (i.e. **population validity** and **ecological validity**).

**Observational studies**
- *Internal validity* may be affected by an inadequate system of **behavioural categories** (e.g. not enough categories) and by **observer bias** (observers' expectations affect their objectivity).
- *Improving internal validity* – Use more than one observer in more than one setting.
- *External validity* – **Naturalistic observations** are likely to have high **ecological validity** but may have low **population validity** when the sample is limited.

**Self-report techniques**
- *Internal validity* may be affected by **interviewer bias** and **social desirability bias**.
- *Improving validity* – Use a more representative **sampling** method and better designed questions.
- *Assessing validity* – Compare the results with an established measure of the same thing (called **concurrent validity**).
- *External validity* – The representativeness of the sample affects the ability to generalise the findings to other people and situations (**population validity** and **ecological validity**).

| Cognitive psychology: Memory | > | Methods and techniques | > | Experiments |
| Developmental psychology: Early social development | > | **Investigation design** | > | Observations |
| **Research methods** | > | Data analysis | | Questionnaires and interviews |
| Biological psychology: Stress | > | and presentation | > | Reliability and validity |
| Social psychology: Social influence | > | | | **Ethical issues** |
| Individual differences: Psychotherapy (abnormality) | > | | | Selection of participants |

## Ethical issues

### Informed consent

- Participants must be given comprehensive information concerning the nature and purpose of a study and their role in it.
- Using this information, participants can make an informed decision about whether to participate.
- From the researcher's point of view this may reduce the meaningfulness of the research because such information will reveal the study's aims and affect participants' behaviour.

### Deception

- This occurs when a participant is not told the true aims of a study and what participation will involve.
- Thus the participants cannot give informed consent.
- From the researcher's point of view it might be argued that some deception is relatively harmless and/or can be compensated for by **debriefing**.

### Right to withdraw

- Participants should have the right to withdraw from a study if they feel uncomfortable in any way.
- They should also have the right to refuse the researcher permission to use any data they produce.
- From the researcher's point of view the loss of participants may bias the study's findings.

### Protection from harm

- During a research study, participants should not experience negative physical effects, such as physical injury, or psychological effects, such as lowered self-esteem or embarrassment.
- From the researcher's point of view it may not be possible to estimate harm before conducting a study – however any study should be stopped as soon as harm is apparent.

### Confidentiality

- A participant's right to have personal information protected.
- The Data Protection Act makes confidentiality a legal right.
- From the researcher's point of view it may not be possible to keep information confidential because details of the study lead to individual's identification.

### Privacy

- A person's right to control the flow of information about themselves.
- From the researcher's point of view this may be difficult, for example in a **covert observation**.
- If privacy is invaded, confidentiality should be protected.

### KEY TERMS

### Ethical issues

- The dilemmas created by the conflict between the needs of researchers and the rights of participants.
- For example, in order to conduct meaningful research it may be necessary to deceive participants, but this affects their right to giving fully informed consent.

## Dealing with ethical issues

### Debriefing

- A post-research interview designed to inform participants about the true nature of a study.
- This aims to restore participants to the state they were in at the start of the study.
- It may also be used to gain feedback about the procedures used in the study.

### Ethical guidelines

- Concrete, quasi-legal documents that help to guide conduct within psychology.
- Establishes principles for standard practice and competence.
- Published by professional organisations such as the *Code of Conduct* produced by the BPS (British Psychological Society).

### Ethical committee (also called institutional review board, IRB)

- A group of people within a research institution that must approve a study before it begins.
- May consist of professionals and lay people.
- Considers how the researcher proposes to deal with any ethical issues that arise.
- Weighs up cost-benefit issues.

### Presumptive consent

- A method of dealing with lack of informed consent or deception.
- Asking a group of people who are similar to the participants whether they would agree to take part in a study.
- If this group of people agree to the procedures in the proposed study, it is presumed that the real participants would agree as well.

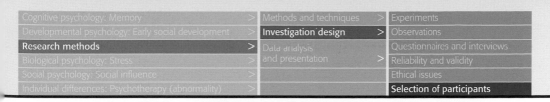

| | | |
|---|---|---|
| Cognitive psychology: Memory | > Methods and techniques | > Experiments |
| Developmental psychology: Early social development | > Investigation design | > Observations |
| **Research methods** | > Data analysis and presentation | Questionnaires and interviews |
| Biological psychology: Stress | > | > Reliability and validity |
| Social psychology: Social influence | > | Ethical issues |
| Individual differences: Psychotherapy (abnormality) | > | **Selection of participants** |

## KEY TERMS

### Attrition
- The loss of participants from a study over time.
- This is likely to leave a biased sample, or a sample that is too small.

### Random technique
- Method of selection that ensures each member of the population has an equal chance of being selected.
- For example, placing all names in a hat and drawing out the required number.
- Or by assigning each person a number and using a random number table.

### Sampling
- The process of taking a sample.
- The technique used aims to produce a representative selection of the target population.

### Target population
- The group of people that the researcher is interested in.
- The group of people from whom a sample is drawn.
- The group of people about whom generalisations can be made.

### Volunteer bias
- A form of sampling bias.
- Occurs because volunteer participants are usually more highly motivated than randomly selected participants.

# Selection of particpants

**Opportunity sample** A sample of participants produced by selecting people who are most easily available at the time of the study.

**How?** Ask people in the street, i.e. select those who are available.

+ The easiest method because you just use the first participants you can find, which means it takes less time to locate your sample than if using one of the other techniques.

− Inevitably biased because the sample is drawn from a small part of the **target population**. For example, if you selected your sample from people walking around the centre of a town on a Monday morning, then it would be unlikely to include professional people (because they are at work), or people from rural areas.

**Random sample** A sample of participants produced using a **random technique** such that every member of the target population has an equal chance of being selected.

**How?** Using a random technique such as placing all names in a hat and drawing out the required number.

+ Unbiased, all members of the target population have an equal chance of selection.

− The researcher may end up with an unrepresentative and therefore biased sample (e.g. more boys than girls) because the sample is too small.

**Stratified and quota sample** Groups of participants are selected according to their frequency in the population.

**How?** Subgroups (or strata) within a population are identified (e.g. boys and girls, or age groups: 10–12 years, 13–15, etc.). Participants are obtained from each of the strata in proportion to their occurrence in the target population. Selection is done randomly (stratified sample) or by another method such as opportunity sampling (quota sample).

+ More representative than an opportunity sample because there is equal representation of subgroups.

− Although the sample represents subgroups, each quota taken may be biased in other ways, for example, if you use opportunity sampling you only have access to certain sections of the target population.

**Systematic sample** A method of obtaining a representative sample by selecting every 5th or 10th person.

**How?** Use a predetermined system to select participants, such as selecting every 10th person from a phonebook.

+ Unbiased as participants are selected using an objective system.

− Not truly random unless you select a number using a random method and start with this person, and then you select every tenth person.

**Volunteer sample** A sample of participants produced by asking for volunteers.

**How?** Advertise in a newspaper or on a noticeboard.

+ Access to a variety of participants (e.g. all the people who read a newspaper) which may make the sample more representative and less biased.

− Sample is biased because participants are likely to be more highly motivated and/or with extra time on their hands (= **volunteer bias**).

Sample

Target population

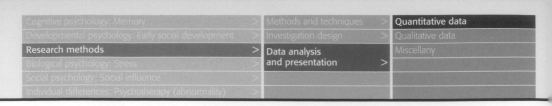

| Cognitive psychology: Memory | > | Methods and techniques | > | Quantitative data |
| Developmental psychology: Early social development | > | Investigation design | > | Qualitative data |
| Research methods | > | Data analysis and presentation | > | Miscellany |
| Biological psychology: Stress | | | | |
| Social psychology: Social influence | | | | |
| Individual differences: Psychotherapy (abnormality) | | | | |

## KEY TERMS

### Quantitative data

- Represent how much, how long, or how many, etc. there are of something.
- Data that are measured in numbers or quantities.

### Quantitative data analysis

- Any means of representing trends from numerical data, such as measures of central tendency.

### Levels of measurement

- **Nominal** Data is in separate categories, such as grouping people according to their favourite football team.
- **Ordinal** Data is ordered in some way, for example asking people to put a list of football teams in order of liking. The 'difference' between each item is not the same, i.e. the individual may like the first item a lot more than the second, but there might only be a small difference between the items ranked second and third.
- **Interval** Data is measured using units of equal intervals, such as when counting correct answers or using any 'public' unit of measurement.
- **Ratio** There is a true zero point as in most measures of physical quantities.

## Quantitative data analysis

 Measures of central tendency

**Measures of central tendency** inform us of central (or middle) values for a data set, i.e. the average.

**Mean** Calculated by adding up all the numbers and dividing by the number of numbers. It can only be used with **interval** or **ratio** data.

+ Makes use of the values of all the data.

− Can be misrepresentative of the data as a whole if there are extreme values.

**Median** The *middle* value in an *ordered* list, suitable for **ordinal** or **interval** data.

+ Not affected by extreme scores.

− Not as 'sensitive' as the mean because not all values are reflected.

**Mode** The value that is *most* common.

+ Useful when the data are in categories, i.e. **nominal** data.

− Not a useful way of describing data when there are several modes (i.e. a multi-modal set of data).

 Measures of dispersion

**Measures of dispersion** inform of us of the spread of the data set.

**Range** The difference between the highest and lowest score in a data set.

+ Easy to calculate, provides you with direct information.

− Affected by extreme values, doesn't take into account the number of observations in the data set.

**Standard deviation** Shows the amount of variation in a data set and assesses the spread of the data around the mean.

+ More precise measure of dispersion because all the values of the data are taken into account.

− May hide some characteristics of the data, for example extreme values.

 Correlation

A **correlational analysis** determines the extent of a relationship between two co-variables.

**Zero correlation** – **Co-variables** are not be linked at all.

**Positive correlation** – Co-variables increase together.

**Negative correlation** – As one co-variable increases, the other decreases. Usually a linear correlation is predicted, but the relationship can be curvilinear.

**Correlation coefficient** A number between −1 and +1 that tells us how closely the co-variables in a correlational analysis are related.

 Visual display

Graphs and tables, such as:

**Bar chart** The height of each bar represents the frequency of that item. The categories are placed on the horizontal (*x* axis) and frequency is on the vertical (*y* axis). Bar charts are suitable for words and numbers (**nominal** or **ordinal/interval** data).

**Scattergram** A graphical representation of the relationship (i.e. the correlation) between two sets of scores.

| | | |
|---|---|---|
| Cognitive psychology: Memory | > Methods and techniques | > Quantitative data |
| Developmental psychology: Early social development | > Investigation design | > **Qualitative data** |
| **Research methods** | > Data analysis | Miscellany |
| Biological psychology: Stress | and presentation | > |
| Social psychology: Social influence | > | |
| Individual differences: Psychotherapy (abnormality) | > | |

## KEY TERMS

### Qualitative data

- Express the 'quality' of things.
- This includes descriptions, words, meanings, pictures, texts and so on.
- They cannot be counted or quantified but it can be turned into **quantitative data** by counting the data in categories.

It is sometimes said that qualitative data concern 'thoughts and feelings' – but you can also have *quantitative* data about thoughts and feelings, for example a researcher could ask participants to rate their feelings about a film on a scale of 1 to 5. The difference between quantitative and qualitative research runs much deeper than 'thoughts and feelings'.

## Qualitative data analysis

**Qualitative** research uses smaller *samples* than quantitative research but usually involves the collection of a large amount of data – pages of written material and/or audio/video recordings. Analysis might involve:

1 Categorising the data. These can be:
   - *Pre-existing categories* – The researcher decides on some appropriate categories before beginning the research.
   - *Emergent categories* – The categories or themes emerge when examining the data.

2 Using the categories to summarise the data.
   - The categories or themes may be listed.
   - Examples of behaviour within the category may be represented using quotes from participants or descriptions of typical behaviours in that category.
   - Frequency of occurrences in each category may be counted, thus qualitative data is turned into quantitative data.
   - Finally, a researcher may draw conclusions.

## Qualitative data versus quantitiative data

| Advantages | Disadvantages |
|---|---|
| **Qualitative data** | |
| • Represents the true complexities of human behaviour.<br>• Gains access to thoughts and feelings that may not be assessed using quantitative methods e.g. **closed questions**.<br>• Provides rich details of how people behave because participants free to express themselves. | • More difficult to detect patterns and draw conclusions because of the large amount of data usually collected.<br>• Subjective analysis can be affected by personal expectations and beliefs – however quantitative methods are also affected by bias; they simply may appear to be objective. |
| **Quantitative data** | |
| • Easier to analyse because the data are given in numbers that can be summarised using measures such as the **mean** and **range**, as well as simple graphs.<br>• Can produce neat conclusions because numerical data reduces the variety of possibilities. | • Oversimplifies reality and human experience (statistically significant but humanly insignificant). |

## Processes involved in content analysis

**Content analysis** is a form of indirect **observation** – indirect because you are not observing people directly but observing them through the artefacts they produce.

The process involved is similar to any observational study, the researcher has to make design decisions about:

1 **Sampling method** – what material to sample and how frequently (e.g. which TV channels to include, how many programmes, what length of time).

2 **Behavioural categories** to be used. These categories can be used in two ways:
   - *Quantitative analysis* – Examples in each category are counted.
   - *Qualitative analysis* – Examples in each category are described rather than counted.

As with observations, if there is a team of researchers it is important to ensure that they are applying criteria in the same way by calculating **inter-observer reliability**.

| Cognitive psychology: Memory | | > | Methods and techniques | > | Quantitative data |
| Developmental psychology: Early social development | | > | Investigation design | > | Qualitative data |
| **Research methods** | | > | Data analysis and presentation | > | Miscellany |
| Biological psychology: Stress | | > | | | |
| Social psychology: Social influence | | > | | | |
| Individual differences: Psychotherapy (abnormality) | | > | | | |

## Other things you should know

**Cohort effects** One group of participants (cohort) may have unique characteristics because of time-specific experiences during their development, such as being a child during the Second World War. This can affect both **cross-sectional studies** (because one group is not comparable with another) or **longitudinal studies** (because the group studied is not typical).

**Conclusions** The implications drawn from a study: what the findings tell us about people in general rather than just about the particular participants in a study. Conclusions are used to construct theories.

**Confederate** An individual in a study who is not a real participant and has been instructed how to behave by the investigator/experimenter. May act as the **independent variable (IV)**.

**Cross-cultural study** A kind of **natural experiment** in which the **IV** is different cultural practices and the **DV** is a behaviour, such as attachment. This enables researchers to investigate the effects of culture/socialisation.

**Cross-sectional study** One group of participants of a young age are compared with another, older group of participants, with a view to finding out the influence of age on the behaviour in question.

**Hawthorne effect** The tendency for participants to alter their behaviour merely as a result of knowing that they are being observed.

**Intervening variable** A variable that comes between two other variables that is used to explain the relationship between those two variables.

**Investigator effect** Anything that the investigator/experimenter does that has an effect on a participant's performance in a study other than what was intended. This includes direct effects (as a consequence of the investigator/experimenter interacting with the participant) and indirect effects (as a consequence of the investigator designing the study).

**Investigator/experimenter bias** The effect that an investigator/experimenter's expectations have on the participants and thus on the results of a research study.

**Longitudinal study** Observation of the same items over a long period of time. Such studies usually aim to compare the same individuals at different ages, in which case the IV is age. A longitudinal study might also observe a school or other institution over a long period of time.

**Meta-analysis** A researcher looks at the findings from a number of different studies in order to reach a general conclusion about a particular hypothesis.

**Participant effects** A general term used to acknowledge the fact that participants react to cues in an experimental situation and that this may affect the **validity** of any conclusions drawn from the investigation.

**Quasi-experiments** Studies that are 'almost' experiments but lack one or more features of a true experiment, such as full experimenter control over the IV and **random allocation** of participants to conditions. This means that they cannot claim to demonstrate causal relationships.

**Role play** A **controlled observation** in which participants are asked to imagine how they would behave in certain situations, and than asked to act out the part. This method has the advantage of permitting a study of certain behaviours that might be unethical or difficult to find in the real world.

**Standardised procedures** A set of procedures that are the same for all participants in order to be able to repeat a study. This includes **standardised instructions** – the instructions given to participants to tell them how to perform a task.

 How science works

The **scientific method** is the method used in scientific research where scientists start by observing natural phenomena and then develop explanations and hypotheses which are tested using systematic research methods.

The **experiment** is the ideal scientific method because it lends itself to being objective and highly controlled, but other methods (such as **observations** and **interviews**) can also be objective and controlled.

# Chapter 4

# Biological psychology

*Column 1: tick when you have produced brief notes.*

*Column 2: tick when you have a good grasp of this topic.*

*Column 3: tick during the final revision when you feel you have complete mastery of the topic.*

| Key terms<br>• **3 marks worth of material** | 1 | 2 | 3 |
| --- | --- | --- | --- |
| Pituitary-adrenal system | | | |
| Sympathomedullary pathway | | | |
| Immune system | | | |
| Stress-related illness | | | |
| Life changes | | | |
| Daily hassles | | | |
| Workplace stressors | | | |
| Type A behaviour | | | |
| Emotion-focused approaches to coping with stress | | | |
| Problem-focused approaches to coping with stress | | | |
| Cognitive Behavioural Therapy | | | |
| **Research studies related to …**<br>• **6 marks worth of description**<br>• **6 marks worth of evaluation (including the issues of reliability, validity and ethics)** | | | |
| The body's response to stress | | | |
| The relationship between the immune system and illness | | | |
| Stress-related illnesses | | | |
| Life changes | | | |
| Daily hassles | | | |
| Workplace stress | | | |
| Personality factors | | | |
| Emotion-focused approaches to coping with stress | | | |
| Problem-focused approaches to coping with stress | | | |
| Psychological methods of stress management | | | |
| Physiological methods of stress management | | | |
| **Factors that affect …**<br>• **6 marks worth of material** | | | |
| Stress | | | |
| Worplace stress | | | |
| **Explanations/theories**<br>• **6 marks worth of description**<br>• **6 marks worth of evaluation (strengths/weaknesses)** | | | |
| The body's response to stress | | | |
| Pituitary-adrenal system | | | |
| Sympathomedullary pathway | | | |
| Stress related illness and the immune system | | | |
| **Applications of stress research**<br>• **6 marks worth of material**<br>• **6 marks worth of evaluation (strengths/weaknesses)** | | | |
| Emotion- and problem-focused approaches to coping with stress | | | |
| **Two** psychological methods of stress management (CBT plus one other) | | | |
| **Two** physiological methods of stress management (two types of drugs) | | | |

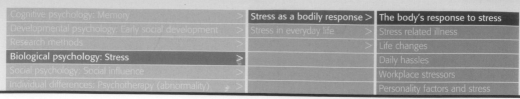

| Cognitive psychology: Memory | > | Stress as a bodily response > | The body's response to stress |
| Developmental psychology: Early social development | > | Stress in everyday life | > | Stress related illness |
| Research methods | > | | > | Life changes |
| Biological psychology: Stress | > | | | Daily hassles |
| Social psychology: Social influence | > | | | Workplace stressors |
| Individual differences: Psychotherapy (abnormality) | > | | | Personality factors and stress |

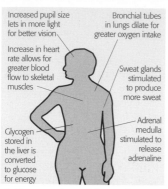

Increased pupil size lets in more light for better vision

Increase in heart rate allows for greater blood flow to skeletal muscles

Bronchial tubes in lungs dilate for greater oxygen intake

Sweat glands stimulated to produce more sweat

Glycogen stored in the liver is converted to glucose for energy

Adrenal medulla stimulated to release adrenaline

▲ *The sympathomedullary pathway (SNS activation)*

## KEY TERMS

### Fight or flight

- A term meaning an animal is energised to either fight or run away in response to a sudden (acute) stressor.

### Pituitary-adrenal system

- Stress response involving the pituitary gland and **adrenal medulla**.
- Helps the body cope with chronic stressors.

### Stress

- When the perceived demands of a situation are greater than the perceived ability to cope.

### Sympathomedullary pathway

- A stress response, involving the **SNS** and **adrenal cortex**, which helps the body prepare for fight or flight.

▼ *The pituitary-adrenal system*

Perception of stressor by higher brain centres

Hypothalamus

**CRF**

Pituitary Gland

**ACTH**

Adrenal Cortex

Negative feedback

**CORT**

Cortisol causes stress effects in the body

# The body's response to stress

 ## Acute stress: The sympathomedullary pathway

**The autonomic nervous system (ANS)** – Immediate (acute) stressors activate the **sympathetic branch** of the ANS. The **sympathetic nervous system (SNS)** prepares the body for **fight or flight**, the rapid action necessary when an animal is under threat. This is achieved by the release of **noradrenaline**, which activates internal body organs associated with fight or flight.

**SNS induced changes** include an increase in heart rate and blood pressure, increased pupil size and metabolic changes, such as the mobilisation of fat and glucose in the bloodstream.

**The adrenal medulla** – A second part of this response to stress involves the adrenal glands, especially the **adrenal medulla**. Neurons of the SNS travel to the medulla, causing it to release **adrenaline** into the bloodstream. Once in the bloodstream, adrenaline boosts the supply of oxygen and glucose to the brain and suppresses non-emergency bodily processes, such as digestion.

 ## Chronic stress: The pituitary-adrenal system

**The hypothalamus** – This response is activated under conditions of chronic (ongoing) stress (see diagram below left). When such stressors are perceived by higher centres in the brain, a message is sent to the **hypothalamus**. Activation of this area leads to the production of **corticotrophin-releasing factor (CRF)**, which is released into the bloodstream.

**The pituitary gland** – On arrival at the **pituitary gland**, CRF causes it to release **adrenocorticotrophic hormone (ACTH)**. This is transported via the bloodstream to the adrenal glands, specifically the **adrenal cortex**.

**The adrenal cortex** – Once activated, the adrenal cortex releases the hormone **cortisol**, which has several effects throughout the body. Some are positive (e.g. lower sensitivity to pain), while some are negative (such as a lowered immune response). Prolonged release of ACTH by the pituitary causes the adrenal cortex to increase in size to produce more cortisol.

## Consequences of the stress response

**Cardiovascular problems** – If these stress responses are repeatedly activated, the heart and blood vessels begin to suffer from abnormal wear and tear. For example, increased blood pressure associated with SNS activation can lead to physical damage in the lining of blood vessels and increase the likelihood of heart disease.

**Immunosuppression** – Too much cortisol suppresses the **immune system**, shutting down the process that fights infection. Under normal conditions, a feedback system triggered by high cortisol levels causes a reduction in CRF and ACTH levels, thus bringing cortisol levels back to normal. This feedback system may break down under conditions of prolonged stress.

### ⏺ PUTTING IT ALL TOGETHER

The stressors we typically face today are different from those faced by early humans. Therefore, the stress responses described above may not be universally adaptive under conditions of stress, and may actually be **maladaptive**.

| Cognitive psychology: Memory | > | Stress as a bodily response > | The body's response to stress |
|---|---|---|---|
| Developmental psychology: Early social development | > | Stress in everyday life | > | **Stress related illness** |
| Research methods | > | | > | Life changes |
| **Biological psychology: Stress** | > | | | Daily hassles |
| Social psychology: Social influence | > | | | Workplace stressors |
| Individual differences: Psychotherapy (abnormality) | > | | | Personality factors and stress |

## KEY TERMS

### Immune system

- Designed to defend the body against **antigens** (bacteria, viruses, toxins, etc.) that would otherwise invade it.
- White blood cells (**leucocytes**) identify and eliminate foreign bodies (antigens).
- The **sympathomedullary pathway** has a direct effect on the immune system – the **ANS** sends nerves directly into the tissues that form and store cells of the immune system.
- The **pituitary-adrenal system** increases levels of circulating **cortisol**, with too much cortisol suppressing the immune system.

## Stress-related illness: Cardiovascular disorders

Stress can lead to **cardiovascular disorders** (disorders of the heart and circulatory system).

- **SNS** activation leads to constriction of blood vessels and a rise in blood pressure and heart rate.
- An increase in heart rate may wear away the lining of blood vessels.
- Stress leads to increased glucose levels in the bloodstream, which may block blood vessels (**atheroschlerosis**).

**The role of anger** – Some people respond to stress with greater feelings of anger. **Williams** asked 13,000 people to complete an anger **questionnaire**. Six years later their health was checked. Those scoring highest on the anger scale were also far more likely to have had a heart attack during that period.

**Work-stress** – **Russek** compared doctors in low-stress occupations (dermatologists and pathologists) with those in high-stress occupations (GPs and anaesthetists). The incidence of cardiovascular disorder was greatest among GPs and lowest among dermatologists, supporting the claim that work stress contributes to illness.

# Stress related illness and the immune system

 key**STUDIES** Kiecolt-Glaser *et al.*

### Acute stressors: Examination stress (Kiecolt-Glaser *et al.*, 1984)

**How?** Method – **natural experiment** with students. The researchers assessed **immune system** functioning one month before an exam and during the exam period itself.

**Showed?** Immune system activity was significantly reduced from a blood sample taken *during* the examination period compared to one taken one month *before*. This suggests that short-term stressors reduce immune system functioning.

**Validity?** Students may not constitute a representative group, however research with other groups exposed to acute stressors has found similar results.

### Chronic stressors: Relationship stress (Kiecolt-Glaser *et al.*, 2005)

**How?** Method – **lab experiment** with married couples, looking at the effects of unhappy relationships.

**Showed?** They found that blister wounds on the arms of couples who showed high levels of hostile behaviour during interactions healed at 60% of the rate of those couples who showed low levels of hostility.

**Validity?** Because this is a lab-based study, it might lack real-life relevance. However, use of such methodologies to explore the association between relationship stress and illness provides clinically relevant data over a relatively short period of time.

 other**RESEARCH**

**Segerstrom and Miller** conducted a **meta-analysis** of 293 studies found that short-term acute stressors could actually boost the immune system, prompting it to prepare itself for infections or injuries. Long-term chronic stressors however, led to suppression of the immune system.

 Evaluation of the stress-immune system relationship

There are various reasons why it is difficult to establish a causal relationship.

1. Health is affected by many different factors (genetics, lifestyle, etc.) therefore there is little variance left to be accounted for by stress.
2. Health tends to be fairly stable and slow to change, therefore it is difficult to demonstrate that exposure to particular stressors have caused a change in health.
3. To demonstrate exposure to stress and health changes over the long-term is impractical, therefore researchers have concentrated on the impact of relatively short-term stressors.

 Individual**DIFFERENCES**

Women show more adverse immunological changes in the way they react to chronic stressors such as marital conflict (**Kiecolt-Glaser *et al.***).

As people age, stress has a greater effect on immune system functioning, making it harder for the body to regulate itself (**Segerstrom and Miller**).

### ⌒ PUTTING IT ALL TOGETHER

The immune system can fail us by being *under-vigilant*, letting infections enter the body, or *over-vigilant*, so that it is the immune system itself that causes illness. Stress might be associated with both these types of immune dysfunction.

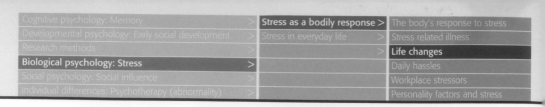

| | | Stress as a bodily response > | The body's response to stress |
|---|---|---|---|
| Cognitive psychology: Memory | > | Stress in everyday life > | Stress related illness |
| Developmental psychology: Early social development | > | > | **Life changes** |
| Research methods | > | | Daily hassles |
| **Biological psychology: Stress** | > | | Workplace stressors |
| Social psychology: Social influence | > | | Personality factors and stress |
| Individual differences: Psychotherapy (abnormality) | > | | |

## KEY TERMS

### Life changes

- Events (e.g. divorce or bereavement) that require a significant adjustment in a person's life.
- A significant source of **stress**.

### SRRS

- Developed by **Holmes and Rahe** to be able to test the idea that life changes are related to stress-related illnesses, such as **anxiety** and **depression**.
- The social readjustment rating scale is based on 43 life events taken from an analysis of over 5000 patient records.
- Marriage is given a 'readjustment' score (life change unit, LCU) of 50.
- Events requiring more readjustment have a LCU higher than 50 and those requiring less have a LCU lower than 50.
- Highest LCU for a life event was death of a spouse (LCU of 100).

 Validity and reliability of research findings

**Validity** – There are concerns over the accuracy of people's memories for life events. People who are unwell may feel a need to provide an explanation for their illness and so are more likely to report stressful events that might have caused it.

**Reliability** – There are also issues over the consistency of retrospective reports, with **Rahe** finding that **test-retest reliability** varies depending on the time interval between testing.

## Life changes as stressors

### keySTUDY Rahe et al. (1970)

**How?** Method – **correlation** using a **questionnaire** (a military version of the **SRRS**) given to 2664 men aboard three US Navy ships. During their six-month tour of duty a record was kept of any illness.

**Showed?** They found a small but significant positive correlation between the men's LCUs over the previous six months and their illness over the same period. As there are both positive and negative events in the SRRS, this appears to indicate that it is not whether a change is considered negative that is important, but the amount of energy required in order to deal with the event that creates stress, and potentially illness.

**Validity?** Research has suggested that a number of variables may moderate the amount of stress associated with life events measured by the SRRS, therefore limiting its usefulness as a universal measure of this relationship.

### otherRESEARCH

**Michael and Ben-Zur** conducted a **natural experiment**. They studied men and women, half recently divorced and half recently widowed. For the bereaved group, levels of life satisfaction were greater *before* and lower *after* bereavement. For the divorced group this was the other way around, with higher levels of life satisfaction after the divorce than before.

What does this show? One possibility is that the divorced group were better able to turn this life change into a positive experience than a negative experience. This was harder for the bereaved group, therefore the negative impact of bereavement was more obvious in this group.

### Evaluation of research findings

**A spurious relationship** – Most studies have yielded only correlational data, failing to demonstrate a *causal* relationship between life events and stress-related illness. It is possible that a third variable affects both.

**IndividualDIFFERENCES** – There are huge individual differences in the impact of life events such as pregnancy, retirement and even relatively minor events such as Christmas or an annual holiday. Because the impact of these events varies from person to person it becomes hard to predict illness from SRRS scores alone.

**Life changes and daily hassles** – Major life changes are relatively rare in most people's lives, so relatively minor **daily hassles** are more likely to be a significant source of stress. **DeLongis et al.** found a significant relationship between health and daily hassles but not for life events.

**Positive and negative events** – Research using the SRRS appears to indicate that *any* life-changing event has the potential to damage health because it requires significant readjustment. Some critics argue that only undesired, unscheduled and uncontrolled changes tend to be *really* harmful.

### PUTTING IT ALL TOGETHER

Events such as the death of a loved one, divorce or a son/daughter leaving home are referred to as *critical* life events because they require a major transition in our lives. As such they can be a major source of stress. However, what might be profoundly stressful for one person, may be a blessed relief for another. Similarly, some life events, such as the death of a much loved pet, can be extremely stressful for some people. As a result, it is difficult to gauge the stressful impact of specific life events as stressors.

| Cognitive psychology: Memory | > | Stress as a bodily response > | The body's response to stress |
| Developmental psychology: Early social development | > | Stress in everyday life | > | Stress related illness |
| Research methods | > | | > | Life changes |
| Biological psychology: Stress | > | | | Daily hassles |
| Social psychology: Social influence | > | | | Workplace stressors |
| Individual differences: Psychotherapy (abnormality) | > | | | Personality factors and stress |

## KEY TERMS

### Daily hassles

- Hassles are those frustrating, irritating everyday experiences that occur regularly in our work, home and personal life.

- For most of us, our life stressors are not major **life changes** like divorce, redundancy or the death of a loved one, but the relatively minor annoyances that affect us more regularly and accumulate over time.

### Daily uplifts

- Uplifts are the minor positive experiences of everyday life that often counter the negative effects of daily hassles.

- They include receiving a compliment at work or feeling good about our appearance.

 **PUTTING IT ALL TOGETHER**

Daily hassles are comparable to, if not greater than, life changes as a significant source of stress. However, the greater negative influence of daily hassles may be due, in part, to the reduced social support received from others, who may be more likely to lend their support when we experience important life changes, but not when we experience daily hassles.

# Daily hassles as stressors

 ResearchEVIDENCE

**Bouteyre et al.** conducted a **correlational analysis** of the relationship between **daily hassles** and mental health in students undergoing the initial transition from school to university. After students completed a hassles questionnaire and a **depression** inventory, the researchers found that over 40% of the new students suffered from depressive symptoms and there was a positive correlation between scores on the hassles scale and the incidence of depressive symptoms.

**Gulian et al.** found that participants who had endured a stressful day at work reported higher levels of **stress** on their journey home. This shows that the effect of daily hassles tends to accumulate over the course of the day. Hassles that haven't been dealt with successfully at the time add to the impact of subsequent stressors.

**Hassles and uplifts – Gervais** asked nurses to keep diaries for a month, recording all the daily hassles and uplifts while at work. After a month, it was clear that daily hassles increased job strain and deceased job performance. However, **daily uplifts** appeared to counteract the stressful impact of these hassles as well as improving job performance.

## Why are hassles so stressful?

**The accumulation effect** – There is an accumulation of minor daily stressors which creates persistent irritations, frustrations and overloads. This then results in more serious stress reactions, such as anxiety and depression.

**The amplification effect** – Chronic stress caused by negative life events may deplete a person's resources, making them more vulnerable to the influence of daily hassles.

**Action theory** – Hassles are disruptive because they involve effort, preventing us from pursuing our primary goals (e.g. getting to work on time). This includes mental effort spent working out how to deal with the hassle as well as physical effort that must be spent actually dealing with it. Because hassles prevent us from reaching our primary goals they can produce negative consequences such as fatigue or bad mood.

## Evaluation

**Memory problems** – Most research on daily hassles has asked participants to assess the impact of hassles experienced over the previous month. The accuracy of such memories tends to vary according to the time interval involved. More recently, researchers have started to overcome this problem using a **diary method** where stressors and feelings are recorded daily.

**Correlations don't show causal relationships** – Even when memories *are* reliable, the data they produce are only correlational. This means that we can't draw causal relationships between daily hassles and our physical and psychological wellbeing. However, correlations do suggest that hassles have the *potential* to have adverse effects on our wellbeing, therefore we would be wise to take them seriously.

**RealWORLD application** – Research in this area gives us an insight into understanding road rage. **Gulian et al.** found that participants who reported a difficult day at work tended to report higher levels of stress on their drive home. When unresolved hassles from the day (e.g. arguments with fellow workers or job-related frustration) were carried forward, events such as the behaviour of other road users were more likely to be interpreted negatively by the stressed driver.

| Cognitive psychology: Memory | > | Stress as a bodily response > | The body's response to stress |
| Developmental psychology: Early social development | > | Stress in everyday life | > | Stress related illness |
| Research methods | > | | > | Life changes |
| **Biological psychology: Stress** | > | | | Daily hassles |
| Social psychology: Social influence | > | | | **Workplace stressors** |
| Individual differences: Psychotherapy (abnormality) | > | | | Personality factors and stress |

## KEY TERMS

### Cardiovascular disorder

- Disorders of the heart or circulatory system, including hypertension (high blood pressure) and heart disease.

### Control

- The degree to which workers perceive that they have control over important aspects of their work, such as deadlines, procedures, etc.

### Role conflict

- This occurs when experiences at work interfere with family life and vice versa (e.g. an employee who always takes work home).
- Or someone whose work performance is affected by their home life.
- Has been shown to be associated with higher levels of absenteeism, lower levels of performance and poorer physical and mental health.

### Workload

- The demands of a person's work role.
- This can be stressful because it is repetitive, high intensity, monotonous or high volume.

### Workplace stressors

- Aspects of our working environment that we experience as stressful, and which cause a stress reaction in our body.

---

### ⓒ PUTTING IT ALL TOGETHER

There are many aspects of the working environment that are commonly reported as being 'stressful'. Each of the types of stressor described on this page has the *potential* to cause a stress reaction, and thus affect physical and psychological health. Whether they do have this effect or not depends on many other factors including an individual's ability to cope and the available social support.

---

## Workplace stressors

 key**STUDY**  Marmot *et al.* (1997)

**How?** – Method – **longitudinal study**. Over seven thousand civil servants were asked to complete a **questionnaire** on **workload**, job control and the amount of social support they received from others. The researchers also checked for signs of **cardiovascular disorder**. Five years later, the participants were reassessed to see if their health status had changed.

**Showed?** The study produced two key results:

- **Workload** – Marmot *et al.* found no link between high workload and stress-related illness, suggesting that workload was not a significant factor in the development of stress-related illness. However, other studies (e.g. **Johansson et al.**) have found that performing repetitive jobs that require high levels of attention and responsibility *were* related to stress-related illness.

- **Control** – Marmot *et al.* found that the civil servants in higher grades developed the fewest cardiovascular diseases and those in the lower grades the most. Those in the higher grades reported greater levels of control over their work and good levels of social support. Those in the lower grades reported less control and had the poorest social support. This suggests that control and social support can moderate the impact of stress.

 other**RESEARCH**

**Pomaki et al.** conducted a **correlational analysis** to investigate the effects of **role conflict** in 226 hospital doctors. The study found that role conflict was directly associated with emotional exhaustion, depressive symptoms and somatic (bodily) complaints.

 Evaluation

**IndividualDIFFERENCES** – **Lazarus'** *transactional approach* to stress emphasises that the degree to which a workplace stressor is perceived as stressful depends on the person's perceived ability to cope. High job demands may be perceived as stressful to one person, but not to another, particularly those high in 'hardiness'. Similarly, **Schaubroeck et al.** found that some people are *less* stressed by having no control or responsibility, and show better **immune responses** in such situations.

**The evolution of work and work stressors** – The nature of the working environment is constantly changing with the advent of new technology and new working practices (including an increase in 'virtual' offices and a blurring of the home work environment). This means that our current knowledge of workplace stressors rapidly becomes out of date. Consequently, psychological research may inevitably lag behind actual work practices.

**Validity** – Many of the studies of workplace stressors have made use of **questionnaires**. However, traditional questionnaires may distort the importance of some items that are no longer important (see point above), while ignoring others that have become a significant source of stress for most people. **Keenan and Newton** used **interviews** in a study of engineers and found that many of the significant stressors mentioned in this study (such as time-wasting job demands) are not included in questionnaires. They conclude that interviews are a more valid way of assessing the impact of workplace stressors than traditional questionnaires.

| Cognitive psychology: Memory | > | Stress as a bodily response | > | The body's response to stress |
| Developmental psychology: Early social development | > | Stress in everyday life | > | Stress related illness |
| Research methods | > | | > | Life changes |
| Biological psychology: Stress | > | | | Daily hassles |
| Social psychology: Social influence | > | | | Workplace stressors |
| Individual differences: Psychotherapy (abnormality) | > | | | **Personality factors and stress** |

## KEY TERMS

**Hardy personality**

- A type of personality, which provides a defence against the negative effects of **stress**.
- A hardy personality is high in control, commitment and challenge.

**Personal Views Survey**

- A measure of 'hardiness'.
- The overall hardiness score is a composite of three subscales: commitment, control and challenge.

**Type A personality**

- A characteristic approach to life.
- Characterised by, for example, competitiveness and impatience.
- It is believed to increase the risk of **coronary heart disease (CHD)**.

### PUTTING IT ALL TOGETHER

Psychology's preoccupation with the Type A personality is, in part, a reflection of the importance of traditional masculinity in the 50s and 60s. As Type A men became aware of the health risks of their lifestyle, hardiness became more important as it emphasised the acquisition of positive health behaviours in men *and* women.

## The Type A personality

**Friedman and Rosenman** described the **Type A personality** as possessing three major characteristics:

- Competitiveness and achievement striving.
- Impatience and time urgency.
- Hostility and aggressiveness.

These are believed to lead to raised blood pressure and an increase in levels of stress hormones.

 **keySTUDY** Friedman and Rosenman (1960)

**How?** Method – a **natural experiment** and **structured interview**, used to assess the personality of 3000 men between the ages of 39 and 59. The questions also assessed the way the men responded to everyday pressures. Participants were classed as Type A or B.

**Showed?** – Eight years later, twice as many (12%) of those who had Type A personalities had died of cardiovascular problems than those who were not classified as Type A. The Type A men also had higher blood pressure and higher levels of cholesterol.

**Validity? Ragland and Brown** carried out a follow up study of Friedman and Roseman's participants 22 years after the start of the study. They found 15% of the men had died of heart disease, but found no relationship between Type A personality and death from **CHD**, challenging the claim that Type A personality was a significant risk factor.

 **other**RESEARCH

**Myrtek** carried out a **meta-analysis** of 35 studies in this area and found an association between CHD and only one component of the Type A personality – hostility. There was no evidence of an association between CHD and other components of the Type A personality.

## The hardy personality

**Kobasa and Maddi** claim that some people are more resistant to the harmful effects of stress because they have a '**hardy personality**' which consists of:

- **Control** – Hardy people see themselves as being in control of their lives rather than being controlled by external factors.
- **Commitment** – Hardy people are involved with the world around them and have a strong sense of purpose.
- **Challenge** – Life challenges are seen as problems to be overcome rather than stressors.

 **keySTUDY** Kobasa (1979)

**How?** The stress scores of 800 business executives were determined using Holmes and Rahe's **SRRS** and hardiness was assessed using a hardiness test.

**Showed?** Kobasa found that 150 of the executives were experiencing high levels of stress. However, these individuals differed in their illness record over the same period. Those with low levels of illness were more likely to have scored high on all three characteristics of the hardy personality and vice versa.

 **other**RESEARCH

**Maddi et al.** measured hardiness in employees of a company that was dramatically reducing its workforce over a period of one year. They found that two-thirds suffered stress-related illness over the year, but the other third thrived, showing evidence of the three components of the hardy personality.

 Evaluation

**Negative affectivity** (NA) may be a simpler explanation. Individuals with high NA dwell more on their failures and on negative aspects of themselves and are more likely to report dissatisfaction and distress.

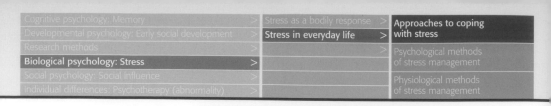

| Cognitive psychology: Memory | > | Stress as a bodily response | > | Approaches to coping with stress |
| Developmental psychology: Early social development | > | Stress in everyday life | > | |
| Research methods | > | | > | Psychological methods of stress management |
| Biological psychology: Stress | > | | | |
| Social psychology: Social influence | > | | | Physiological methods of stress management |
| Individual differences: Psychotherapy (abnormality) | > | | | |

## KEY TERMS

**Emotion-focused coping**
- The use of strategies that deal only with the emotional distress associated with stressful events.

**Problem-focused coping**
- The use of strategies designed to deal directly with the stressful situation itself.

 Individual**DIFFERENCES**

Research has often found that females are more likely to use emotion-focused coping and males problem-focused coping.

**Rosario** suggests two possible reasons for these gender differences:
- **Socialisation theory** – women are taught to express their emotions more openly, whereas males are taught to approach stressful situations with a more active, problem-focused manner.
- **Role constraint theory** – gender differences in coping are a product of the *roles* that males and females tend to occupy.

Rosario found that males and females in the *same* roles tended not to differ in their reported use of problem- or emotion-focused coping, thus supporting the role constraint explanation rather than the socialisation differences explanation.

 **PUTTING IT ALL TOGETHER**

Emotion-focused coping is regarded as a passive process that involves changing thoughts or feelings associated with a stressful event whereas problem-focused coping involves taking direct behavioural action against stressful events.

# Approaches to coping with stress

 ## Problem-focused coping

Common strategies include:
- Taking control of the situation.
- Evaluating pros and cons of different options for dealing with the stressor.
- Suppressing competing activities that might interfere with this.

Problem-focused coping is the more effective coping strategy provided; the individual has a realistic chance of changing those aspects of the situation that are causing them stress.

 ## Emotion-focused coping

Common strategies include:
- Denial and distancing.
- Focusing on and venting emotions.
- Wishful thinking.

People typically use problem-focused coping with events that are potentially controllable, and emotion-focused coping with stressors perceived as less controllable. Emotion-focused coping can reduce physiological arousal levels prior to the use of a more constructive problem-focused approach.

 ## Research**EVIDENCE**

**Penley *et al.*** conducted a **correlational analysis** and showed that problem-focused coping was positively correlated with overall health outcomes, whereas *negative* emotion-focused coping (e.g. avoidance and wishful thinking) was associated with poor overall health outcomes.

**Gilbar**, in a **natural experiment** involving patients diagnosed with breast cancer, found that the use of emotion-focused coping was associated with high levels of psychological distress, while the use of problem-focused coping was beneficial in allaying this distress.

**Folkman and Lazarus** investigated different coping responses used by students. In the run-up to exams, problem-focused coping was more evident, with emotion-focused coping more evident during the wait for results.

 ## Evaluation

**Problems of measurement** – The standard measurement instrument in this research is the *Ways of Coping* measure. However, many of its items are more appropriate to some types of stressor (e.g. relationship stressors) than others (e.g. health problems).

**Is emotion-focused coping always maladaptive?** – Emotion-focused coping may be unhelpful when dealing with certain stressors, for example it may prevent a person from seeking appropriate treatment when they are ill. However, it can be useful during any recovery period, though it can distract the individual from making any necessary lifestyle changes.

**Problem-focused coping isn't for everyone** – **Mullis and Chapman** found that adolescents with high levels of self-esteem used more problem-focused and less emotion-focused coping strategies than adolescents with low levels of self-esteem. This emphasises the importance of positive self-worth among adolescents who must cope effectively with stress in their lives.

| | | |
|---|---|---|
| Cognitive psychology: Memory | Stress as a bodily response > | Approaches to coping with stress |
| Developmental psychology: Early social development | **Stress in everyday life** > | |
| Research methods | > | **Psychological methods of stress management** |
| **Biological psychology: Stress** > | | |
| Social psychology: Social influence | | Physiological methods of stress management |
| Individual differences: Psychotherapy (abnormality) > | | |

## KEY TERMS

### Cognitive Behavioural Therapy (CBT)

- A form of therapy that combines two approaches:
  - Cognitive Therapy which aims to change **maladaptive** thoughts and beliefs.
  - Behavioural Therapy which aims to change behaviour.

### Hardiness training

- The aim of hardiness training is to increase self-confidence and a sense of self-control within an individual's life.

### Stress inoculation training (SIT)

- A type of **CBT** which trains people to cope with stressful situations more effectively by learning skills to protect them from the damaging effects of future stressors.

### ⟲ PUTTING IT ALL TOGETHER

These psychological approaches to stress management are an example of the problem-focused approach to coping. Individuals can change the way they think about problems in their life, or learn techniques that minimise the negative effects of stressful situations.

# Cognitive Behavioural Therapy (CBT)

##  Stress inoculation training

**Meichenbaum** believed that although we can't change the causes of **stress**, we can change the way we think about stressors and the way we react to them. People can be trained to 'inoculate' themselves against a stressor before it arises. The three phases of SIT are:

- **Conceptualisation** – Clients are taught to think differently about stressors, i.e. as problems that can be solved.
- **Skills acquisition** – Coping skills are taught and rehearsed in real life.
- **Application** – Learned coping skills are applied in increasingly stressful situations.

##  Evaluation

### Strengths

1 **Effectiveness – Meichenbaum** compared SIT with **systematic desensitisation** to deal with snake phobias. Both were effective *but* SIT helped to reduce fear associated with a second, as yet untreated phobia.

2 **Sheehy and Horan** found that sessions of SIT reduced anxiety and stress among students over time, as well as improving their academic performance.

3 **Preparation for future stressors** – SIT gives the client the necessary skills so they are less adversely affected by stressors in the future.

### Weaknesses

1 **Time consuming and requires high motivation** – Although SIT has been criticised because of this, Meichenbaum has also demonstrated the effectiveness of relatively brief periods of training.

2 **Unnecessarily complex** – It is possible that effectiveness of SIT can still be achieved with just some of its elements. It may be equally effective to learn how to talk more positively and relax more.

##  Hardiness training

**Kobasa and Maddi** identified a personality type that was especially resistant to stress – the **hardy personality** (see page 35). They believed that people could be trained in **hardiness**, to help them manage stress better.

Hardiness training involves:

- **Focusing** – The client is taught to recognise the sources of stress and the physiological signs of stress.
- **Reliving stress encounters** – The client is given an insight into current coping strategies by reliving previous encounters and their response to them.
- **Self-improvement** – These insights can be used to move forward and learn new techniques, e.g. seeing stressors as challenges they can take control of rather than problems they must give in to.

## ⬡ Evaluation

### Strengths

1 **It works** – Hardiness training has been shown to be effective in many different populations. It has been shown to help at-risk students to deal with the stresses they face during their college life.

2 **RealWORLD application** – Hardiness training has been used to increase commitment to training in Olympic swimmers, by helping to control aspects of their daily lives that might interfere with training schedules (**Lancer**).

### Weakness

1 **Overcoming bad habits** – Training must first address basic aspects of personality and learned habits of coping that are difficult to modify, therefore hardiness training cannot be seen as a rapid solution to management.

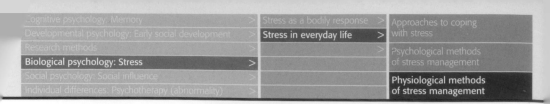

| Cognitive psychology: Memory | > | Stress as a bodily response | > | Approaches to coping with stress |
| Developmental psychology: Early social development | > | **Stress in everyday life** | > | |
| Research methods | > | | > | Psychological methods of stress management |
| **Biological psychology: Stress** | > | | | |
| Social psychology: Social influence | > | | | Physiological methods of stress management |
| Individual differences: Psychotherapy (abnormality) | > | | | |

## KEY TERMS

### Benzodiazepines

- A group of drugs (e.g. *Librium* or *Valium*) used to treat anxiety and stress.
- Works by slowing down the activity of the **central nervous system**.

### Beta-blockers

- Decrease **anxiety** by reducing the activity of **adrenaline/ noradrenaline**.
- These are released as part of the body's response to **stress**.

### Placebo

- A drug or treatment that contains no active ingredient or therapeutic procedure.

### Withdrawal symptoms

- Abnormal physical or psychological reactions to the abrupt discontinuation of a drug to which an individual has developed physical dependence.

*Sending neuron*
*Receiving neuron*
*Synaptic gap*
*Neurotransmitter substance*
*Receptor site on dendrite of receiving neuron*

▲ *GABA is released from one neuron across the **synaptic gap** where it reacts with special receptors with the second receiving neuron. BZs are carried to special booster sites on these receptors, where they enhance the action of GABA.*

### ↻ PUTTING IT ALL TOGETHER

Physiological methods of stress management are a form of emotion-focused coping because they focus on alleviating the emotions associated with the stressful situation rather than dealing with the situation itself.

## Drug therapies

###  Benzodiazepines (BZs)

**Benzodiazepines** are drugs that are used to treat the anxiety that is a consequence of stress. They do this by slowing down the activity of the central nervous system. How do they achieve this?

- **GABA** is a **neurotransmitter** that is the body's natural form of anxiety relief. GABA has a natural quietening effect on many of the **neurons** in the brain by indirectly making it harder for them to be stimulated by other neurotransmitters, slowing down their activity and making the person feel more relaxed.
- BZs enhance the action of GABA, making neurons in the brain even more resistant to excitation and making the person feel much calmer.

###  Beta-blockers (BBs)

**Beta-blockers** are drugs that reduce the activity of **adrenaline** and **noradrenaline** which are part of the **sympathomedullary** response to stress. Thus BBs can prevent some of the **cardiovascular** problems associated with chronic levels of stress. How do they achieve this?

- BBs reduce the activity of adrenaline and noradrenaline by binding to receptors on the cells of the heart and other parts of the body that are usually stimulated during arousal.
- By blocking these receptors, it is harder to stimulate these cells, so the heart beats slower and with less force, blood pressure falls, and so on. As a result, the person feels calmer and less anxious.

###  ResearchEVIDENCE

**Kahn et al.** conducted an **experiment** where a group of patients were given a drug and another group given a **placebo**. This enabled them to see if the success of a drug in reducing symptoms was attributable to its pharmacological properties or to something psychological. They followed 250 patients for eight weeks. BZs were significantly superior at reducing anxiety compared to placebo.

**Hildalgo et al.** conducted a **meta-analysis** and found that BZs were more effective than other drugs for reducing anxiety.

###  Evaluation

#### Strengths

1 **Effectiveness**, as illustrated by the research evidence above.
2 **Ease of use** – Drug treatments require little effort from the patient compared to the significant investment in time and motivation required in the psychological methods discussed on the previous page.

#### Weaknesses

1 **Addiction** – Patients exhibit **withdrawal symptoms** when they stop taking BZs, indicating a psychological dependence, hence use of BZs is recommended to be limited to just four weeks.
2 **Side effects** – For BZs, these include increased aggressiveness and impairment of memory. Some studies have linked BBs to an increased risk of developing developmental diabetes.
3 **Treating the symptoms rather than the problem** – Effectiveness of drug treatments for stress and anxiety only lasts as long as the person takes the drug because the problem itself has not been addressed.

# Chapter 5

# Social psychology

*Column 1: tick when you have produced brief notes.*

*Column 2: tick when you have a good grasp of this topic.*

*Column 3: tick during the final revision when you feel you have complete mastery of the topic.*

| Key terms<br>• **3 marks worth of material** | 1 | 2 | 3 |
|---|---|---|---|
| Conformity | | | |
| Internalisation | | | |
| Compliance | | | |
| Informational social influence | | | |
| Normative social influence | | | |
| Obedience | | | |
| Independent behaviour | | | |
| Locus of control | | | |
| **Research studies related to …**<br>• **6 marks worth of description**<br>• **6 marks worth of evaluation (including the issues of reliability, validity and ethics)** | | | |
| Conformity | | | |
| Internalisation | | | |
| Compliance | | | |
| Informational social influence | | | |
| Normative social influence | | | |
| Obedience | | | |
| How people resist pressures to conform | | | |
| How people resist pressures to obey authority | | | |
| Influence of locus of control on independent behaviour | | | |
| **Factors that affect …**<br>• **6 marks worth of material** | | | |
| Conformity | | | |
| Internalisation | | | |
| Compliance | | | |
| Obedience | | | |
| Independent behaviour (individual differences) | | | |
| **Explanations/theories**<br>• **6 marks worth of description**<br>• **6 marks worth of evaluation (both strengths and weaknesses)** | | | |
| Conformity | | | |
| Why people obey | | | |
| How people resist pressures to conform | | | |
| How people resist pressures to obey authority | | | |
| Independent behaviour | | | |
| Influence of locus of control on independent behaviour | | | |
| **Applications of social influence research**<br>• **6 marks worth of material** | | | |
| Independent behaviour | | | |
| Implications of research into conformity for social change | | | |
| Implications of research into obedience for social change | | | |
| Implications of research into independent behaviour for social change | | | |

| | | |
|---|---|---|
| Cognitive psychology: Memory | **Social influence** | **Conformity to majority influence** |
| Developmental psychology: Early social development | Social influence in everyday life | Conformity to minority influence |
| Research methods | | Explanations of why people conform |
| Biological psychology: Stress | | Obedience |
| Social psychology: Social influence | | Explanations of why people obey |
| Individual differences: Psychotherapy (abnormality) | | |

## KEY TERMS

### Conformity
- A form of social influence.
- Results from exposure to the **majority position**.
- Leads to compliance with that position.
- The tendency for people to adopt the behaviour and attitudes of other members of their group.

 Types of conformity

Kelman proposed three types of **conformity**:

**Compliance** – going along with others to gain their approval or avoid their disapproval. This is a result of social comparison, which enables an individual to adjust their behaviour to that of the group. There is no change in the person's underlying attitude, only their public behaviour.

**Internalisation** – going along with others because of an acceptance of their point of view. This is a result of an examination of the group's position, which may lead to *validation* of the person's own views, or acceptance of the group's views both in public and in private.

**Identification** – going along with others because of a desire to be like them. By adopting the attitudes and behaviours of others, an individual feels more a part of the group, and is more likely to be accepted by them.

 **PUTTING IT ALL TOGETHER**

Conforming to the views or behaviours of others may be a consequence of different psychological motivations (the need to be liked, the desire to be right). Results of the Asch study are primarily the result of the very human need to be accepted by others, therefore can be explained in terms of *compliance*, i.e. a change in public behaviour only.

## Conformity to majority influence

 Key**STUDY** Asch (1956)

**How?** Method – **lab experiment**, 123 male American undergraduates volunteered to take part in a test of their 'vision', although, unbeknown to these volunteers, all the other participants were **confederates** of the experimenter. Asch showed a series of lines to the participants seated around a table. Each, in turn, had to state out loud which of three comparison lines were the same length as a standard line. The real participant always answered last or second to last. On 12 of the 18 trials, the confederates were instructed to give the same incorrect answer.

**Showed?** On the 12 trials where confederates gave the same wrong answer, 36.8% of the responses given by the real participants were also incorrect (i.e. they conformed to the decision of the group). Only 25% of participants never conformed at all. Without confederates giving the wrong answers, participants were correct in their judgments 99% of the time.

**Variations of this study** showed that when the task was made more difficult, conformity increased, that the size of the majority was relatively important (provided it was over three) but that unanimity was vital otherwise conformity dropped away almost completely.

 Evaluation

**A child of its time? Perrin and Spencer** had difficulty getting the same scale of conformity in their 1980 replication, although they subsequently acheived this if they made the perceived costs of *not* conforming appear high. They concluded that Asch got the results he did because in 1956, America was in the grip of McCarthyism, a strong anti-Communist period when people were scared to be different.

**Conformity or independence?** An often overlooked fact is that on two-thirds of the trials where the majority gave the same *wrong* answer, the participant stuck to their original opinion. This suggests that rather than being overly conformist, human beings are able to display **independent behaviour** even in the face of an overwhelming majority.

**Culture and conformity**. A **meta-analysis** of studies of conformity across 17 countries by **Smith and Bond** established that **collectivist cultures** show significantly higher levels of conformity than **individualist cultures**. Level of conformity also declined steadily since Asch's research, with the date of the study negatively correlated with the level of conformity found in the study. However, cultures are not homogenous in terms of individualist and collectivist values, so drawing conclusions based on differences *between* cultures is an oversimplification.

 Individual**DIFFERENCES**

**Eagly and Carli** carried out a meta-analysis of studies and found that women are generally more compliant than men. However, they also found that male researchers were much more likely to find gender differences than female researchers, possibly because they used experimental materials that were more familiar to males than to females.

 Validity

Asking people to judge the length of lines is a trivial task, and people may well be willing to conform simply to save face. On a more important task, we might expect conformity levels to drop. **Baron et al.** found that when the task was difficult, conformity levels increased in line with task importance but on easy tasks conformity levels *decreased* with increased task importance.

## KEY TERMS

### Minority influence

- A form of social influence.
- Where people reject the established norm of the majority of group members and move to the position of the minority.
- In contrast with **majority influence**, minority influence is more likely to lead to **internalisation** rather than **compliance**.

 Conclusions

**Nemeth** suggests

1. Minorities can promote a different viewpoint, but must be consistent to be influential.
2. Even if they are consistent, only rarely do minorities prevail. They tend to be disliked, seen as incompetent and rejected by members of the majority.
3. Exposure to a minority viewpoint stimulates members of the majority to be more creative problem solvers by showing all sides of an issue.

---

⟳ **PUTTING IT ALL TOGETHER**

In order for minority influence to take place, there must be conversion within individuals who were formerly part of the majority. This involves careful thinking through of the arguments of the minority and the gradual internalisation of its point of view. As a result, the process of internalisation tends to be relatively slow, whereas conformity to majority influence is a far more rapid and passive process, as individuals comply with the majority position without a great deal of thought.

---

# Conformity to minority influence

 Key**STUDY** Moscovici *et al.* (1969)

**How?** Method – **lab experiment**. Participants. 32 groups of six women. In each group, two women were **confederates** and four were real participants. They were shown 36 blue slides, each a slightly different shade of blue. Participants had to describe the colour of each slide as it was presented. In one condition, the confederates consistently described each slide as 'green', and in another they answered 'green' 24 times and 'blue' 12 times (i.e. they were inconsistent). In a control group, participants answered without any influence from the confederates.

**Showed?** The real participants went along with the minority on 8.42% of the trials when they were consistent in their judgments, but this dropped to 1.25% when the minority was inconsistent. Thirty two percent went along with the minority at least once (i.e. described a blue slide as green). When participants were allowed to write down their judgments rather than saying them aloud, their agreement with the minority increased. This suggests that part of the inhibition of minority influence is people's reluctance to be seen as aligning themselves with a deviant minority in public.

 Research**EVIDENCE**

**Wood *et al.*** carried out a **meta-analysis** of 97 studies of minority influence, and confirmed that:

- Minorities perceived as consistent were most influential.
- Majority group members avoided aligning themselves with a deviant minority because they did not want to be seen as deviant themselves.
- Majority group members were more likely to admit being influenced by the minority privately rather than publicly.

 Explaining minority influence

**Conversion theory** – When an individual is exposed to an argument that contradicts their own views, this creates a conflict. They are motivated to reduce this conflict, and so examine the views of the minority more closely to understand *why* these people do not hold the same opinions as they do. As a result, the individual concentrates on the *content* the minority's arguments, which means that there is the possibility that their views will be **internalised**. In contrast, when exposed to the opinions of a majority, there is no need to do this, and any change in opinion is due solely to the relationship between the individual and the group (i.e. **compliance**).

 Evaluating minority influence

**Majority rather than minority influence** – **Mackie** argues that in fact it is the *majority* who are more likely to create greater message processing because of the **false consensus effect** (the belief that the majority of group members share similar beliefs). If the majority expresses a view that is different from that of an individual, they must consider it carefully to understand *why* it is different. In contrast, people tend not to waste time trying to process why a minority's message is different.

**Validity** – The relevance of minority influence *beyond* the laboratory is not that clear-cut. **Kalven and Zeisel** suggest that among juries, it is the *majority* view at the time deliberation begins that tends to determine the final verdict. **Mackie** claims that discussion does take place in democratic politics, but change (i.e. conversion) is relatively rare.

| | | |
|---|---|---|
| Cognitive psychology: Memory | Social influence | Conformity to majority influence |
| Developmental psychology: Early social development | Social influence in everyday life | Conformity to minority influence |
| Research methods | | **Explanations of why people conform** |
| Biological psychology: Stress | | Obedience |
| **Social psychology: Social influence** | | Explanations of why people obey |
| Individual differences: Psychotherapy (abnormality) | | |

## KEY TERMS

**Normative social influence**

- The result of wanting to be liked and be accepted by a group.
- This results in a decision to follow group norms.
- Tends to result in **compliance**.

**Informational social influence**

- The result of wanting to be right.
- Believing that the majority has the right answer.
- Conforming to their opinion.
- Tends to result in **internalisation**.

**Social impact theory**

- States that the likelihood that a person will respond to social influence will increase with three factors:
  - *Strength* – how important an influencing group is.
  - *Immediacy* – how close a group is.
  - *Number* – how many members a group has.

# Explanations of conformity

 Normative social influence

This happens when an individual acts in the same way as the majority without actually *accepting* their point of view. It is conformity in action alone, and is also known as **compliance**. Because humans are a social species, they have a strong desire to be accepted and a fear of rejection. This makes it difficult for them to deviate from the majority, because of the risk of rejection. This fear forms the basis of normative social influence.

**ResearchEVIDENCE** The power of normative social influence has been demonstrated in a study on buying. **Garandeau and Cillessen** showed how children with a low level of friendships can be manipulated by a skilful bully so that victimising another child provides the group with a common goal. This puts pressure on group members to comply to maintain the friendship of the other members of the group.

 Informational social influence

In other cases, individuals may go along with the majority because they genuinely believe them to be right, i.e. they have more information than the individual has about that particular issue. This tends to result in the individual conforming in both behaviour *and* attitude (i.e. both public and private change), therefore is an example of **internalisation**.
Informational social influence is most likely when:

- The situation is ambiguous, i.e. the right course of action is not clear.
- The situation is a crisis, i.e. rapid action is required.
- We believe others to be experts, i.e. we believe that others are more likely to know what to do.

**ResearchEVIDENCE** has supported the important role that informational social influence plays in shaping opinion. For example, **Fein *et al.*** showed how judgments of candidate performance in US presidential debates could be influenced by knowledge of the reactions of the majority. Participants who saw on screen what they thought were the reactions of fellow participants during the debate shifted their judgment of the candidates' performance in the direction of what they thought was the majority opinion.

 Social impact theory (Latané, 1981)

This theory aims to explain why people conform in some situations but not others. The likelihood of conformity is determined by the following factors:

- **Number** – The more people present, the more influence they will have on the individual. However, beyond a certain point, the rate of impact associated with a growth in majority size decreases.
- **Strength** – The more important members of the majority are to the individual, the more influence the majority will have over them. For example, in research by **Perrin and Spencer**, when the majority was composed of probation officers and the individual was a person on probation, conformity rates were relatively high.
- **Immediacy** – We are more influenced by others that are more immediate to us. For example, we are more likely to conform to those with whom we interact regularly or those living close to us, rather than those with whom we rarely interact or that live farther away.

⟳ **PUTTING IT ALL TOGETHER**

People conform for many reasons, ranging from complete acceptance of the majority viewpoint (i.e. internalisation), to 'going along' with the crowd (compliance). Two explanations are normative social influence, when we follow the crowd, and informational social influence, when we accept the majority viewpoint because it is most likely to be right.

## KEY TERMS

### Obedience to authority

- A type of social influence.
- Somebody acts in response to a direct order from a figure with perceived authority.
- There is also the implication that the person receiving the order is made to respond in a way that they would not have done without the order.

**Maximum shock level administered**

Location moved to run down office — 48%
Teacher in same room as learner — 40%
Teacher presses learner's hand on shock plate — 30%
Experimenter gives orders over phone — 21%
Another 'teacher' refuses to give shocks — 10%

0  10  20  30  40  50
%

## PUTTING IT ALL TOGETHER

In this form of social influence, the individual is faced with the choice of whether to comply with a direct order from a person with higher status or whether to defy the order. The ethics of Milgram's study have been questioned as has its validity as a representation of real-life obedience. Zimbardo claims that the reason why Milgram's research has attracted so much hostile criticism is because of *what* he discovered, not because of *how* he discovered it.

# Obedience

 Key**STUDY** Milgram (1963)

**How?** Method – **lab experiment**, varying different situational pressures to see which had the greatest effect on obedience.

- Forty male volunteers were told it was a study of how punishment affects learning.
- After drawing lots (which was rigged), the real participant was assigned the role of 'teacher'. The learner was a **confederate**.
- The teacher's job was to administrate a learning task and deliver 'electric shocks' to the learner (in another room) if he got a question wrong.
- The shocks began at 15 volts and increased in increments of 15 volts to a maximum of 450 volts.

**Showed?** All participants went to at least 300 volts, with only 12.5% stopping at that point. An astonishing 65% of the participants continued to the maximum 450 volts, showing high levels of obedience.

 Milgram's variations

**Milgram** conducted variations to the original study (see graph on left) and found the following:

**Proximity of the victim** (e.g. they could be seen) decreased obedience, presumably because it removed the psychological **buffer** between action (giving shocks) and consequence. With the learner in the same room as the participant, obedience levels dropped to 40%. In the touch proximity condition, obedience levels dropped to 30%.

**Proximity of authority figure** made participants feel they were being monitored, so obedience levels were high. When the experimenter left the room and gave orders over the telephone, participants felt better able to defy, and obedience levels dropped to 21%.

**Presence of allies** – In the two peers rebel study, two confederates shared the teacher's role with the real participant. When they refused to carry on, almost all participants also withdrew.

 Evaluation

### Ethics

- **Deception and lack of informed consent** – Participants were misled by being told the experiment was about the effects of punishment on learning rather than its true purpose (obedience). Consequently, participants were effectively denied the right to informed consent.
- **Protection from psychological harm** – **Baumrind** claimed that Milgram had placed his participants under great emotional strain, causing psychological damage that could not be justified. In his defence, Milgram argued that post-study interviews found no evidence of such harm.

**Internal validity** – **Orne and Holland** claim that people have learned to distrust experimenters in psychology because they know the real purpose of the experiment is likely to be disguised. Consequently, participants must have known they were not giving real shocks, particularly when the experimenter appeared completely unconcerned over the learner's cries of pain.

**External validity** – **Mandel** argued that Milgram's conclusions about the situational determinants of obedience in situations such as the Holocaust are not borne out by real-life events, and quotes **Browning**'s study of Reserve Police Battalion 101 at Josefow to support this assertion.

| | | Social influence | Conformity to majority influence |
|---|---|---|---|
| Cognitive psychology: Memory | | | |
| Developmental psychology: Early social development | | Social influence in everyday life | Conformity to minority influence |
| Research methods | | | Explanations of why people conform |
| Biological psychology: Stress | | | Obedience |
| Social psychology: Social influence | | | Explanations of why people obey |
| Individual differences: Psychotherapy (abnormality) | | | |

**PUTTING IT ALL TOGETHER**

Milgram was able to demonstrate the power of the situation in shaping behaviour, with moral constraints such as conscience and compassion being sidelined when an individual is confronted with a powerful authority figure.

# Explanations of obedience

 Gradual commitment

In **Milgram's** study, participants have already committed themselves to giving lower level shocks, and therefore it is harder to resist the experimenter's requirement to give shocks at a higher level. As the transition from one shock level to another is very gradual (15 volt increments), it becomes even harder for participants to change their minds about continuing. This is an example of what psychologists call the 'foot in the door' approach, once someone signals their willingness to agree to a small request, their ability to refuse larger requests from the same source diminishes.

 Agentic shift

Milgram argued that people shift back and forwards between an **autonomous state**, where they see themselves as responsible for their own actions, and an **agentic state**, where they see themselves as an agent for carrying out the instructions of another person. When they perceive themselves as receiving an order from someone in authority, they shift from the former to the latter.

 The role of buffers

In Milgram's base-line study, the 'teacher' and 'learner' were in separate rooms, therefore, when the teacher delivered an electric shock they did not have to witness the consequences. **Buffers** such as physical distance therefore protect the individual from at least some of the distress they may otherwise experience when they carry out actions that harm another person.

 Evaluating explanations of obedience

**Mandel** claims that Milgram's explanation of obedience, particularly when applied to the Holocaust, is oversimplified and misleading.

**Monocausal emphasis – Mandel** suggests that by focusing solely on obedience as an explanation for the atrocities carried out in the Holocaust, Milgram ignored many other plausible explanations. Goldhagen argues that **anti-Semitism** was the primary motivation for these acts, and that Germans did not need the pressure of authority to allow them to discriminate against, and ultimately kill, Jews.

**Agentic shift** – It is inappropriate to draw parallels between Milgram's lab and Holocaust events. Holocaust perpetrators carried out their duties over years, yet Milgram's participants were involved for just half an hour. There is also a difference in their perception of harm-doing, with Holocaust perpetrators *knowing* they were causing harm, whereas Milgram's participants were assured there would be no permanent damage.

**Consequences of an obedience alibi** – By attributing Holocaust events to obedience, Mandel argues that:

- The suggestion that Holocaust perpetrators were 'just obeying orders' is distressing for all those whose lives were affected by the Holocaust.

- Such an explanation effectively exonerates war criminals of their crimes.

**RealWORLD application** – Insights from Milgram's research can help us understand some of the abusive behaviour of guards at the Abu Ghraib prison in Iraq. For example, in Milgram's study gradual commitment was one of the most important determinants of obedience. The prisoner abuses observed in Abu Ghraib were also gradual in nature, coupled with the presence of compliant peers and an apparently unconcerned authority figure.

| Cognitive psychology: Memory | Social influence | Independent behaviour |
| Developmental psychology: Early social development | Social influence in everyday life | Individual differences in independent behaviour |
| Research methods | | Implications for social change |
| Biological psychology: Stress | | |
| Social psychology: Social influence | | |
| Individual differences: Psychotherapy (abnormality) | | |

## KEY TERMS

### Anticonformity

- The refusal or failure to conform to the generally accepted standards, conventions or rules of a group.

### Heroic imagination

A mental orientation that involves:

- Imagining facing potentially risky situations (e.g. pressure to conform to an antisocial behaviour).
- Struggling with the hypothetical problems these situations raise.
- Considering one's likely actions and their consequences.

### Independence

- Behaving in a way that shows freedom from any control or influence of other group members.

## RealWORLD application

Research suggests specific actions that people can take to resist pressure to obey:

- **Ask – 'Is this something I would do *without* an order?**
  Reawakening personal moral considerations makes resistance more likely.

- **Beware of the 'foot in the door'** – Agreeing to a small initial request makes it harder to resist later larger requests.

- **Find an ally** – The presence of an ally makes defiance appear easier and more legitimate.

# Independent behaviour – Resisting social influence

## Resisting conformity

**The role of allies – Asch** showed how the introduction of another person who went against the majority caused conformity rates to drop significantly, but why?

A fellow dissenter provides the individual with an assessment of reality, making them more confident in their own decision. Conformity levels dropped even when the dissenter gave a *wrong* answer. This suggests that it is breaking the group's consensus that is important in increasing resistance.

**Moral considerations** – People are likely to conform to a majority position even though they know the majority position is wrong. The costs of conforming in Asch's study are not particularly great given the insignificance of the task, and the benefits are significant (not looking foolish). However, if the task involves a moral dimension (e.g. cheating), there is less evidence of conformity as the costs of such conformity are significantly greater.

**The nonconformist personality** – Individuals who respond to **majority influence** with **independence** (i.e. they give the right answer rather than agreeing with the majority's wrong answer) tend to be less concerned with social norms.

Some individuals are predisposed to react to majority influence by actively opposing the norm, *whatever* it is. They may be fully aware of the norm but choose to oppose it, showing an **anticonformity** dimension to their personality.

## Resisting obedience

**Status** – When **Milgram's** study was moved from the prestigious setting of Yale University to a downtown office, more participants felt able to resist the experimenter. This tells us that status of the authority figure is a key factor in obedience and its resistance.

**Proximity** – Resistance was also increased when the victim could be seen, or when other **confederates** were present. This shows that being made aware of the effects of obedient actions and having social support makes it more likely that the individual will feel able to resist pressures to obey.

**Moral considerations**
**Kohlberg** interviewed participants who had obeyed the experimenter and those who had resisted. He found that those who based their decision on more advanced moral principles (e.g. the importance of justice over social order) were more defiant, whereas those who obeyed the experimenter completely tended to reason at a lower moral stage.

**Social heroism – Zimbardo** argues that while the majority of individuals would bow to the demands of an unjust authority, there are others who feel able to resist regardless of the consequences. He describes them as displaying **social heroism**, e.g. Nelson Mandela, jailed for opposing apartheid in South Africa. Zimbardo believes that a key factor in social heroism is stimulation of the **heroic imagination**, a mental orientation that makes it more likely that people will be able to resist an unjust authority figure and act 'heroically' when the time comes.

## PUTTING IT ALL TOGETHER

We have seen on the last few spreads how situational factors tend to increase the likelihood that people will conform or to obey. It is evident that in order to *resist* these pressures, individual factors must take precedence over situational factors. These include acting in line with personal moral considerations, having a personality that make mindless conformity less likely and the development of a heroic imagination.

| Cognitive psychology: Memory | | Social influence | Independent behaviour |
| Developmental psychology: Early social development | | Social influence in everyday life | Individual differences in independent behaviour |
| Research methods | | | |
| Biological psychology: Stress | | | Implications for social change |
| Social psychology: Social influence | | | |
| Individual differences: Psychotherapy (abnormality) | | | |

**Attribution**

- When observing behaviour (our own or someone else's) we provide explanations for the behaviour.
- These explanations will be **dispositional** or **situational**.

**Attributional style**

- A personality attribute.
- Indicates how people consistently explain to themselves why they experience a particular type of event.

**Locus of control**

- An aspect of our personality.
- People differ in their causal beliefs.
- The outcomes of their actions are contingent on either:
  - what they are or what they do (internal control, **internals**) or
  - events outside their personal control (external control, **externals**).

# IndividualDIFFERENCES in independent behaviour

 Locus of control

This refers to a person's perception of the degree of personal control they have over their behaviour.

- High **internals** perceive themselves as having a great deal of personal control over their behaviour, so take more responsibility for it.
- High **externals** perceive their behaviour as being caused more by external influences or luck, therefore take less personal responsibility for it.

Individuals who are low in externality (i.e. high in internality) are more likely to display independent behaviour. For example:

- High internals are active seekers of information and rely less on the opinions of others.
- High internals are better able to resist coercion from others.

 Evaluation

**ResearchEVIDENCE –**
**Twenge et al.** carried out a **meta-analysis** on young Americans, and found that locus of control scores had become substantially more external between 1960 and 2002. The consequences of this trend are worrying, because high externality is associated with decreased self control, poor school achievement and depression.

**Reasons for the trend** – The rise in social factors such as the divorce rate, violent crimes, etc. over this period has led many young people to see some aspects of their lives as beyond their control.

 Attributional style

When people experience success or failure in what they do, they make causal **attributions** for these events. The consistency with which they make specific types of attributions determines their **attributional style**.

- **Personal** – People may see themselves as the cause of events (**dispositional**) or may attribute the cause to external factors (**situational**).
- **Permanent** – An individual may see the situation (e.g. failure at a task) as either changeable (i.e. the result can be different next time) or unchangeable.
- **Pervasive** – An individual may see an event as affecting *all* aspects of their life, or having a more restricted 'local' influence.

 Positive and negative

**Positive attributional style** – Does not let negative events affect other aspects of their life, synonymous with **independent behaviour** as they are able to resist influence of negative life experiences.

**Negative attributional style** – Blame themselves for negative events, believe these will last indefinitely and let them affect many aspects of their lives.

 Evaluation

**ResearchEVIDENCE** – Students who were more rebellious at school were found to have experienced more negative experiences and had consequently developed a negative attributional style (**Heaven et al.**).

 IndividualDIFFERENCES

**Locus of control** – **Rotter** claims that people high in internality rely more on their own actions and exhibit greater initiative, making them more successful. **Linz and Semykina** used a **questionnaire** to collect data from over 2600 Russian employees. Although there was no relationship between earnings (a measure of success) for men, there was for women. Internals were the highest wage earners.

**Attributional style** – **Anderson** measured attributional style, **depression** and loneliness in Chinese and American students. Chinese students accepted more responsibility for failures and less credit for successes than did US students. This relatively **maladaptive** attributional style was associated with higher scores for depression and loneliness in the Chinese students.

 **PUTTING IT ALL TOGETHER**

The concept of locus of control distinguishes between *internals* – people who attribute the cause of events in their life to their own control, and *externals* – who locate control outside themselves and so tend to feel they have less control over what happens to them.

| Cognitive psychology: Memory | | Social influence | Independent behaviour |
| Developmental psychology: Early social development | | Social influence in everyday life | Individual differences in independent behaviour |
| Research methods | | | |
| Biological psychology: Stress | | | Implications for social change |
| Social psychology: Social influence | | | |
| Individual differences: Psychotherapy (abnormality) | | | |

## KEY TERMS

### Civil disobedience

- A group's refusal to obey a law because they believe the law is immoral.

### Social change

- Occurs when a society as a whole adopts a new belief or way of behaving.
- This then becomes widely accepted as the norm.

### Terrorism

- Any act intended to cause death or serious bodily harm to civilians.
- With the purpose of intimidating a population or compelling a government to do, or abstain from, doing any act.

 Validity

**Blass** carried out a **correlational analysis** of all of Milgram's obedience experiments, and the replications carried out by other researchers between 1961 and 1985 to see whether obedience levels dropped over time. He found no such correlation; later studies found no more or less obedience than earlier studies. This indicates that Milgram's studies of obedience still appear to be as relevant to social change as they were nearly 50 years ago.

### ⏱ PUTTING IT ALL TOGETHER

Some forms of social influence can be a force for positive social change (e.g. Gandhi's non-violent protests against the British salt tax in India in the 1930s). It can also be a force for negative social change (e.g. the Nazi extermination of Jews during World War II was made easier by the tendency for those involved to obey their superiors).

# Implications for social change

Social influence might be thought of as synonymous with social control, but many of the insights derived from this research can be used to bring about **social change**.

##  Conformity research

**From minority to majority** – We have seen how **minorities** can influence members of the **majority** to change their opinions if the message is persuasive, and the minority is consistent in their advocacy of it. The minority is then transformed into the new majority. However, groups with changed minority and majority positions may suffer an exodus of group members from both minority *and* the new majority factions. For example, in South Africa after power was transferred to black South Africans, few members of the majority black population reported improvement in their lives, and the new white minority reported a significant deterioration, leading to an increase in emigration from both groups.

**Peaceful minorities** – Non-violent minorities such as the followers of Gandhi in India in the 1930s and the civil rights movement in America in the 1960s were successful in bringing about social change because they were *consistent* in their message, and their influence was increased by their willingness to suffer without retaliation.

**Terrorism as a tactic of social change** – **Kruglanski** argues that **terrorism** might be considered a form of social change through the process of minority influence. Research into minority influence has shown that the influence of a minority is most effective when it is consistent. Terrorist attacks in Afghanistan and Iraq are *consistent*, and those concerned often demonstrate a lack of concern for the consequences of their actions *for them* (e.g. suicide bombers). Terrorism may draw attention to the legitimacy of the minority faction's claims and lead to **internalisation** of their position.

## ⬡ Obedience research

Power depends on continuing obedience. If people refuse to obey, then power crumbles. Social change can, therefore, be achieved through *dis*obedience.

**Disobedient models** – In a variation of his obedience study, **Milgram** placed the participant with two **confederates** who defied the experimenter and refused to punish the learner against his will. In this variation, 36 of the 40 participants also defied the experimenter. Parallels to this have been found in many real-life examples of **civil disobedience** including Nelson Mandela (anti-apartheid, South Africa) and Rosa Parks (civil rights movement, USA).

**A 'drift to goodness'** – **Zimbardo** believes that we can use the same principles that define obedience to produce a drift to goodness rather than a drift to evil. In Milgram's studies, participants initially gave only a 15-volt shock, and then found it difficult not to continue to 450 volts. Psychologists have also found that asking people to do something small and helpful to start with made it more likely that they would help in more significant ways later on.

**Obedience as a mechanism of social change** – Obedience itself can be the process by which a group brings about social change. During the **Holocaust**, many Nazis claimed that they were 'only obeying orders' to bring about the particular form of social change favoured by the Nazi leadership, the total elimination of European Jews and the development of a pure 'master race'. Similarly, during the Rwandan genocide in 1994, many Hutu obeyed orders to rid Rwanda of the Tutsi minority.

# CHAPTER 6

# Individual differences

*Column 1: tick when you have produced brief notes.*

*Column 2: tick when you have a good grasp of this topic.*

*Column 3: tick during the final revision when you feel you have complete mastery of the topic.*

| Key terms<br>• **3 marks worth of material**<br>• **Limitations associated with each definition** | 1 | 2 | 3 |
|---|---|---|---|
| Deviation from social norms | | | |
| Failure to function adequately | | | |
| Deviation from ideal mental health | | | |
| **Research studies related to …**<br>• **6 marks worth of description**<br>• **6 marks worth of evaluation (including the issues of reliability, validity and ethics)** | | | |
| Drug therapy | | | |
| ECT | | | |
| Psychoanalysis | | | |
| Systematic desensitisation | | | |
| Cognitive Behavioural Therapy | | | |
| **Explanations/theories**<br>• **6 marks worth of description**<br>• **6 marks worth of evaluation (both strengths and weaknesses)** | | | |
| Deviation from social norms | | | |
| Failure to function adequately | | | |
| Deviation from ideal mental health | | | |
| Biological approach to psychopathology | | | |
| Psychological approach: Psychodynamic model | | | |
| Psychological approach: Behavioural model | | | |
| Psychological approach: Cognitive model | | | |
| Drug therapy | | | |
| ECT | | | |
| Psychoanalysis | | | |
| Systematic desensitisation | | | |
| Cognitive Behavioural Therapy | | | |

| Cognitive psychology: Memory | Defining and explaining psychological abnormality | Definitions of abnormality |
| Developmental psychology: Early social development | | The biological approach |
| Research methods | Treating abnormality | The psychodynamic approach |
| Biological psychology: Stress | | The behavioural approach |
| Social psychology: Social influence | | The cognitive approach |
| Individual differences: Psychotherapy (abnormality) | | |

## KEY TERMS

**Cultural relativism**

- The view that ideas of normal and abnormal behaviour differ from culture to culture.

**Deviation from ideal mental health**

- Abnormality is seen as deviating from an ideal of positive mental health.
- This includes a positive attitude toward the self and an accurate perception of reality.

**Deviation from social norms**

- Abnormal behaviour is a deviation from unwritten rules about how one 'ought' to behave.
- Violation of these rules is considered abnormal.

**Failure to function adequately**

- Mentally healthy people are judged as being able to operate within certain acceptable limits.
- If abnormal behaviour interferes with daily functioning, it may be considered abnormal.

 **PUTTING IT ALL TOGETHER**

All these definitions have their problems, therefore the definition of abnormality inevitably remains a subjective judgement. Consequently, abnormality is usually determined by the presence of several of these characteristics at the same time rather than one alone.

# Definitions of abnormality

##  Deviation from social norms

All societies have social norms – standards of acceptable behaviour such as politeness, appropriate sexual behaviour, etc. These are not formal laws but implicit (i.e. unwritten) rules concerning what people expect from the behaviour of others. People who behave in a socially deviant way (i.e. they display behaviour that breaks these unwritten rules) are considered anti-social or undesirable – therefore *abnormal* – by the rest of the group.

### Limitations of the deviation from social norms definition

**Deviance is related to context and degree** – Judgments of deviance are dependent on the *context* of a behaviour. Some behaviours are considered acceptable in one context but not in another. There is also no clear line between what is an abnormal deviation and what is harmless eccentricity.

**Cultural relativism** – Any attempt to define a behaviour as abnormal is futile without also considering the culture in which it occurs. What is considered a diagnosable disorder and therefore 'abnormal' in one culture may be considered acceptable and therefore 'normal' in another. This means there are no universal standards for labeling a behaviour as abnormal.

##  Failure to function adequately

From an individual's point of view, abnormality can be judged in terms of 'not being able to cope'. Feeling **depressed** does not become a problem for the individual until their depression begins to interfere with their ability to cope with day-to-day living. When this happens, people may label their own behaviour as abnormal and seek treatment.

### Limitations of the failure to function adequately definition

**Adaptive or maladaptive?** – Some behaviours that *appear* dysfunctional and abnormal may actually be adaptive for the individual. For example, depression may lead to welcome extra attention for the individual, which helps them deal with the stressor that led to the depression in the first place.

**Cultural relativism** – Definitions of adequate functioning are also related to cultural ideals of how one's life should be lived. This means that the 'failure to function adequately' criterion of abnormality is likely to result in different diagnoses when applied to people from different cultures because the standard of one culture is being used to measure another.

## Deviation from ideal mental health

**Jahoda** identified six characteristics of ideal mental health, such as:
- *Self-attitudes* – positive self-esteem and a strong sense of identity.
- *Integration* – being able to deal with stressful events.
- *Accurate perception of reality*.

This definition proposes that the *absence* of these criteria indicates abnormality and a potential mental disorder.

### Limitations of the deviation from ideal mental health definition

**Who can achieve all these criteria?** – According to this definition, all of us are abnormal to some degree, as it is unusual to find people that satisfy all the criteria all of the time.

**Cultural relativism** – Most of these criteria are culture-bound. If we apply them to non-Western cultures, we will probably find a higher incidence of abnormality. Some criteria, such as **self-actualisation**, are relevant to members of **individualist cultures** but not members of **collectivist cultures**.

| Cognitive psychology: Memory | | Defining and explaining psychological abnormality | Definitions of abnormality |
| Developmental psychology: Early social development | | | The biological approach |
| Research methods | | Treating abnormality | The psychodynamic approach |
| Biological psychology: Stress | | | The behavioural approach |
| Social psychology: Social influence | | | The cognitive approach |
| Individual differences: Psychotherapy (abnormality) | | | |

## KEY TERMS

### Biological approach to psychopathology

- Explains behaviour in terms of physiological and/or genetic causes.
- A mental disorder represents the consequences of a malfunction of biological processes.

### Concordance rates

- A measure of similarity between two individuals or sets of individuals on a given trait.
- Usually expressed as a percentage.

### Diathesis-stress model

- In the case of certain disorders, individuals inherit a vulnerability for the disorder (diathesis).
- The disorder only develops if such individuals are exposed to difficult environmental conditions (**stress**).
- The greater the underlying vulnerability, the less stress is needed to trigger the disorder.

### Genetic inheritance

- The reception of genetically coded traits as a result of transmission from parent to offspring.

### Neuroanatomy

- The branch of anatomy that deals with the structure of the brain and other parts of the nervous system.

### Neurochemistry

- The action of chemicals (e.g. **neurotransmitters**) in the brain and the drugs that influence neural activity.

## Key features of the biological approach

**Abnormality is caused by physical factors** – The **biological approach to psychopathology** assumes that, like physical disorders, mental disorders are related to change, illness or dysfunction in the body.

**Genetic inheritance** – Abnormalities in brain anatomy (**neuroanatomy**) or brain chemistry (**neurochemistry**) are a product of **genetic inheritance** and so are passed from parent to child. **Concordance rates** are a way of measuring the extent to which two individuals are alike in terms of a specific trait (such as **schizophrenia**). If identical twins display high concordance rates for a mental disorder, such as schizophrenia, then it suggests a significant genetic influence is at work.

**Neuroanatomy and neurochemistry** – Abnormalities in the structure of the brain may determine abnormality. For example, some schizophrenics have enlarged spaces (ventricles) in their brains, indicating shrinkage of the brain tissue around the ventricles. Altered brain chemistry can lead to abnormal behaviour, e.g. low levels of **serotonin** have been found in the brains of individuals suffering from **depression**.

**Viral infection** – Some disorders may be explained by exposure to viruses in the womb. Research has found that mothers of some schizophrenics have contracted a strain of the influenza virus during pregnancy. The virus is thought to enter the unborn child's brain, remaining dormant until puberty.

 Limitations of the biological approach

**Humane or inhumane?** The emergence of a biological approach to abnormality meant that mental illness could be treated. However, **Szasz** suggested that the concept of 'mental illness' was invented merely to control (through drugs or hospitalisation) those individuals who society could not accept as they are. He argued that unlike physical illnesses, most mental disorders did not have a physical basis, therefore could not be treated in the same way.

**Inconclusive evidence** – If mental disorders are caused by genetic factors alone, then concordance rates would be 100% for that mental disorder. In twin studies of schizophrenia, the concordance is only about 50%, suggesting that environmental influences are equally important. It is possible that what is inherited is a vulnerability to the disorder (a diathesis), which only develops under certain stressful conditions (**diathesis-stress model**).

**Cause or effect?** There isn't a simple cause and effect relationship between biological influences and mental disorders. Research has shown that some schizophrenics have enlarged ventricles, but it is not clear whether these are the cause of schizophrenic symptoms or a consequence of them (e.g. the result of taking medication to treat schizophrenia).

### ⟳ PUTTING IT ALL TOGETHER

One of the advantages of this approach is that its ideas can be tested scientifically. For example, biochemical explanations can be tested using experiments that alter levels of a specific neurotransmitter in the brain. If symptoms improve (compared to those in a **placebo** condition), this supports the influence of biochemical factors.

| Cognitive psychology: Memory | Defining and explaining psychological abnormality | Definitions of abnormality |
| Developmental psychology: Early social development | | The biological approach |
| Research methods | Treating abnormality | **The psychodynamic approach** |
| Biological psychology: Stress | | The behavioural approach |
| Social psychology: Social influence | | The cognitive approach |
| Individual differences: Psychotherapy (abnormality) | | |

## KEY TERMS

### Ego

- The conscious, rational part of a personality.
- Develops because a young child must deal with the constraints of reality and so is governed by the **reality principle**.

### Ego defences

- Unconscious methods, such as repression and projection, which help protect an individual from feelings of anxiety.

### Id

- The irrational, primitive part of a personality.
- Demands immediate satisfaction and is ruled by the **pleasure principle**.

### Oedipal conflict

- Incestuous feelings that a young boy develops for his mother, coupled with rivalry with the father for her affections, leading to castration anxiety.
- Resolution of this conflict leads to the development of the superego.

### Psychodynamic approach to psychopathology

- Any approach that emphasises the dynamics of behaviour.
- In other words, what *drives* us to behave in particular ways.

### Superego

- Develops between the ages of three and six.
- Embodies our conscience and sense of right and wrong, as well as notions of the ideal self.

# Key features of the psychodynamic approach

**Mental disorders have psychological not physical causes** – **Freud**'s **psychodynamic approach to psychopathology** believed that mental illnesses were not physical in origin but were the result of unresolved childhood conflicts.

Conflicts between the **id**, **ego** and **superego** create anxiety. This can be relieved by the use of **ego defences** such as **repression** (moving unpleasant thoughts into the unconscious), **projection** (blaming someone else for something a child cannot deal with) and **regression** (behaving like a child when faced with a difficult situation). These unconscious defences can be the cause of disturbed behaviour if they are overused.

**Early experiences cause mental disorder** – In childhood, the ego is not mature enough to deal with traumas such as the loss of a parent, so this may lead to repression of any associated emotions. Later in life, further losses may cause the individual to re-experience this earlier loss, leading to **depression**.

**Unconscious motivations and mental disorder** – The unconscious mind exerts a powerful effect on behaviour through the influence of previously repressed emotions or trauma. This frequently leads to distress, as the individual does not understand why they are acting in that particular way. The underlying problem cannot be controlled until it is brought into conscious awareness.

##  Limitations of the psychodynamic approach

**Abstract concepts** – Concepts such as the id, ego and superego are abstract and therefore difficult to define and to demonstrate through research. Because conflicts between these three aspects of the personality operate at a primarily, unconscious level, there is no way to know for certain that they are operating. As a result, psychodynamic explanations of psychopathology have received little empirical (i.e. research) support.

**Lack of research support** – The theory is difficult to prove or disprove using scientific methodology, therefore much of the support is from **case studies**. However, **Fisher and Greenberg** reviewed over 2,500 **experimental** studies of Freudian hypotheses, and discovered that many of Freud's major claims received experimental support. A problem for research into psychoanalysis is that positive results are taken as supporting the hypothesis, but negative results are often also used as support because, it can be argued that, defence mechanisms disguise the real underlying conflict.

**Sexism** – Freud's theory is sexually unbalanced (e.g. his emphasis on the **Oedipal conflict** in boys which, he claimed, led to superior moral development). However, this is not surprising given that Freud himself was male, and at the time he was writing, the cultural bias meant that women were considered less significant than men. Nonetheless, this does limit the relevance of this approach to understanding the development of mental disorders in women.

 **PUTTING IT ALL TOGETHER**

Psychodynamic theorists believe that an individual's abnormal behaviour is determined by underlying psychological conflicts of which they are largely unaware (i.e. they are the product of unconscious forces). The best-known psychodynamic theorist is Freud. He believed that unconscious forces determined all normal *and* abnormal behaviour.

| | | |
|---|---|---|
| Cognitive psychology: Memory | **Defining and explaining psychological abnormality** | Definitions of abnormality |
| Developmental psychology: Early social development | | The biological approach |
| Research methods | Treating abnormality | The psychodynamic approach |
| Biological psychology: Stress | | **The behavioural approach** |
| Social psychology: Social influence | | The cognitive approach |
| Individual differences: Psychotherapy (abnormality) | | |

## KEY TERMS

### Behavioural approach to psychopathology

- Behaviourists believe that normal *and* abnormal behaviours are acquired as a result of experiences that we have in life.
- Abnormal behaviours are learned through the processes of **classical** and **operant conditioning** and **social learning**.

### Maladaptive behaviour

- Behaviours that inhibit a person's ability to cope with, or adjust to, particular situations.

### Social learning theory

- The assumption that people learn through indirect as well as direct rewards by observing the behaviour of models (**observational learning**).
- And then imitating such behaviour if others have been rewarded for such behaviour (**vicarious reinforcement**).

## Key features of the behavioural approach

**Only behaviour is important** – The **behavioural approach** focuses only on *behaviours*; the observable responses that a person makes to their environment. For example, someone with **obsessive-compulsive disorder** might display compulsive behaviours such as constant hand washing, or someone with a **phobia** (phobic disorder) may display extreme **anxiety** in the presence of the phobic object.

**Abnormal behaviours are learned** – Abnormal behaviour is no different to normal behaviour in terms of how it is learned.

- For example, a psychological disorder might be produced when a **maladaptive behaviour** (such as a panic attack) leads to the desired increased attention for the individual (**operant conditioning**).
- Abnormal behaviours may also be acquired by seeing others rewarded for the same behaviour (**social learning theory**).

**Learning environments** – The environments in which behaviours are learned may reinforce maladaptive behaviours.

- For example, for an individual with **agoraphobia**, not leaving home lowers anxiety, and for those with **depression**, depressive behaviours may elicit help from others.
- Therefore, such behaviours may be learned because they are actually *adaptive* for the individual in those environments.

 Limitations of the behavioural approach

**A limited view** – Behaviourist explanations have been criticised for offering an extremely limited view of the factors that might cause abnormal behaviours. Behaviourist explanations tend to ignore the role of physiological or cognitive factors in the onset and treatment of abnormality, both of which have been shown to have an important role to play in both the emergence of psychopathology and in its treatment.

**Counter evidence** – One of the strengths of this approach is that it lends itself to scientific validation. However, research does not always support its claims. For example, explanations of the acquisition of phobic behaviours that focus on the role of conditioning in the development of these behaviours struggle to explain why so many people with a phobia cannot recall an incident in their past which led to traumatic conditioning or even any contact with the feared object.

**The symptoms not the cause** – Part of the success of this approach comes from the effectiveness of behavioural therapies for treating abnormal behaviour. However, such therapies treat only the symptoms, and the cause may still remain and simply resurface, albeit in a different form. This suggests that although the *symptoms* of many disorders are behavioural, the *cause* may not be.

## PUTTING IT ALL TOGETHER

Behaviourists believe that our actions are determined largely by the experiences we have in life, rather than by underlying pathology (the biological approach) or unconscious forces (the psychodynamic approach). Abnormality is seen as the development of behaviour patterns (through conditioning or through social learning) that are considered maladaptive for the individual.

| Cognitive psychology: Memory | | Defining and explaining psychological abnormality | Definitions of abnormality |
| Developmental psychology: Early social development | | | The biological approach |
| Research methods | | Treating abnormality | The psychodynamic approach |
| Biological psychology: Stress | | | The behavioural approach |
| Social psychology: Social influence | | | **The cognitive approach** |
| Individual differences: Psychotherapy (abnormality) | | | |

▲ *The cognitive model emphasises the importance of cognitive processing in psychological adjustment. The sleeping dog, whose real nature is unknown, is seen differently by two cats.*

## KEY TERMS

### A-B-C model

- Refers to the three components of experience that can be used to judge whether an individual's belief system is distorted.
- A for activating event – an event that we might encounter and can describe objectively.
- B for belief – what an individual believes is the truth about an event. This might include predictions about what any consequences might be.
- C for consequences – the feelings experienced as a result of beliefs associated with an event.

### Cognitive approach to psychopathology

- Psychopathological behaviour is explained in terms of irrational and negative thinking about the world.
- If this faulty thinking can be changed, the problem will disappear.

### Cognitive distortions

- Dysfunctional thought processes.
- For example processing information in a way likely to cause anxiety, or drawing faulty conclusions after processing information.

## Key features of the cognitive approach

**Abnormality is caused by faulty thinking** – The **cognitive approach to psychopathology** assumes that thinking, expectations and attitudes (i.e. cognitions) direct behaviour.

- Mental illness is the result of **cognitive distortions** in the way a person thinks about a problem.
- Faulty and irrational thinking prevents the individual behaving adaptively.

**The A-B-C model** (**Ellis**, 1962)

- **A** refers to an **activating event** (e.g. the sight of a large dog).
- **B** is the **belief**, which may be rational (e.g. 'the dog is harmless') or irrational (e.g. 'the dog will attack me').
- **C** is the **consequence** – rational beliefs lead to healthy emotions (e.g. amusement) and irrational beliefs lead to unhealthy emotions (e.g. fear).

**The individual is in control** – Unlike the other three models, where abnormal behaviour is thought to be *determined* by factors outside the individual's control (e.g. **genetic** or environmental factors), the cognitive model portrays the individual as being the cause of their own behaviour, because they control their own thoughts. Abnormality is the result of faulty control of this process.

 Limitations of the cognitive approach

**Blames the patient** – The cognitive model suggests it is the patient who is responsible, therefore overlooks situational factors, such as situational stressors. By focusing only on events in the patient's mind, the implication is that recovery is only possible by changing the way the person thinks about these stressors, rather than changing the stressors themselves. Research on stress suggests that complete recovery must also target the sources of stress in a person's life.

**Consequence rather than cause** – It is not clear which comes first, i.e. do **maladaptive** thoughts cause mental disorder, or does mental disorder lead to faulty thinking? It is possible that an individual develops a negative way of thinking because of their disorder (as happens in depression). It is also possible that faulty thinking is a vulnerability factor for psychopathology, with individuals with maladaptive cognitions being at greater risk of developing mental disorders.

**Irrational beliefs may be realistic** – Not all irrational beliefs are 'irrational'. **Alloy and Abrahmson** suggest that many **depressives** actually have a much more realistic view of the world than non-depressives. They found that depressed people gave much more accurate estimates of the likelihood of a disaster than 'normal' controls (the 'sadder but wiser' effect).

 **PUTTING IT ALL TOGETHER**

The cognitive model of psychopathology emphasises that cognitive distortions may be at the root of many psychological disorders, particularly those that involve irrational and negative thinking. Distortions in the way we process information have been implicated in depression, **schizophrenia** and other mental disorders.

| Cognitive psychology: Memory | Defining and explaining | **Biological therapies** |
| Developmental psychology: Early social development | psychological abnormality | Psychological therapies |
| Research methods | **Treating abnormality** | |
| Biological psychology: Stress | | |
| Social psychology: Social influence | | |
| **Individual differences: Psychotherapy (abnormality)** | | |

## KEY TERMS

**Antipsychotics**
- Drugs that are effective in the treatment of psychotic illnesses, such as schizophrenia.

**Benzodiazepines (BZs)**
- Drugs that have a tranquillising effect and are commonly used in the treatment of anxiety.

**Beta-blockers (BBs)**
- Drugs that block the action of adrenaline and noradrenaline during **sympathetic arousal**.

**ECT**
- Electro-convulsive shock therapy.
- The administration of an electrical current through electrodes on the scalp.
- Induces a seizure, which can be effective in relieving an episode of major depression.

**SSRIs**
- Selective serotonin re-uptake inhibitors, a class of drug used in the treatment of **depression**.

## ⟳ PUTTING IT ALL TOGETHER

The biological approach proposes that the cause of psychopathology lies in underlying physiological processes, so it makes sense for the treatment to also be physical. Thus, biological therapies target physiological processes, such as the functioning of neurotransmitters, hormones and parts of the brain.

# Biological therapies

##  Chemotherapy

**Antipsychotic drugs** are used to combat the symptoms of psychotic illnesses such as **schizophrenia**. Conventional **antipsychotics** block the transmission of **dopamine**, and so alleviate many of the symptoms of this disorder.

**Antidepressant drugs** – **SSRIs** work by blocking the transporter mechanism that reabsorbs **serotonin** into the nerve cell, thus prolonging its activity and relieving symptoms of depression.

**Anti-anxiety drugs** – **Benzodiazepines** reduce anxiety by slowing down activity of the central nervous system. **Beta-blockers** reduce the activity of **adrenaline** and **noradrenaline**, part of the body's response to stress.

##  Strengths

**Effectiveness** – Research suggests that chemotherapies do work when compared to **placebo** conditions. However, drugs alone are less effective than drugs combined with psychological therapies.

**Ease of use** – Drug therapies require little effort from the patient, therefore they are likely to be more motivated to continue treatment compared to more time-consuming psychological treatments.

##  Limitations

**Tackle symptoms rather than cause** – Drugs only offer temporary alleviation of symptoms. As soon as the patient stops taking the drug, its effectiveness ceases and the symptoms return.

**Side effects** – All drugs have side effects, e.g. SSRIs can cause nausea and suicidal thoughts. This is one of the main reasons drug treatments fail, as patients stop taking their medication because they can no longer stand the side effects.

##  ECT

**ECT** is generally used for severely **depressed** patients for whom psychotherapy and drug medication have proved ineffective.

**How does it work?** A small amount of electric current, lasting about half a second, is passed through the brain. This current produces a seizure, which affects the whole brain.

**Why does it work?** ECT causes changes in the way the brain works, but there is disagreement about the exact effects that lead to improvement. ECT affects the action of **neurotransmitters**, so recovery from depression may be a consequence of improving communication between different parts of the brain.

##  Strengths

**ECT can save lives** – ECT can be an effective treatment, particularly in cases of severe depression. As a result, it can be life-saving, particularly when depression is so severe that it could lead to suicide.

**Effectiveness** – **Comer** states that 60–70% of ECT patients improve after treatment, although critics have also suggested that 84% of these patients had relapsed within six months of receiving ECT.

##  Limitations

**Sham ECT** – Studies that have compared the use of 'sham' ECT with real ECT have found that those receiving real ECT were more likely to recover. Some sham patients also recovered, suggesting that attention plays a part in recovery.

**Side effects** – Possible side effects include impaired memory, **cardiovascular** problems and headaches. A report from the **DOH** found that for those receiving ECT over the previous two years, 30% reported that it had left them with permanent fear and anxiety.

| Cognitive psychology: Memory | Defining and explaining psychological abnormality | Biological therapies |
| Developmental psychology: Early social development | | **Psychological therapies 1** |
| Research methods | **Treating abnormality** | Psychological therapies 2 |
| Biological psychology: Stress | | |
| Social psychology: Social influence | | |
| Individual differences: Psychotherapy (abnormality) | | |

## KEY TERMS

### False memories

- Remembering events, especially traumatic events, that have not actually occurred.
- May be prompted by the suggestion of a therapist.

### Neurotic illness

- Describes a **nonpsychotic** mental illness that triggers feelings of distress and **anxiety** and impairs functioning.

### Psychoanalysis

- A therapy developed by Sigmund Freud to make the unconscious conscious and deal with the causes of abnormal behaviour.
- Individuals are generally unaware of the many factors, some of which are unconscious, that cause their behaviour and affect their mental health.

### Spontaneous remission

- The disappearance of psychopathological symptoms over time without formal treatment.

 Ethics

Psychoanalysis as a therapy is potentially fraught with **ethical** problems. These include the stress of *insight,* as painful memories are brought into the conscious mind, and the controversy of *false memories* (see right).

 **PUTTING IT ALL TOGETHER**

The psychological approach to treatment focuses more on psychological dimensions of behaviour (how people think and feel) than does the biological approach. Psychoanalysis attempts to help patients become aware of long-repressed unconscious feelings and issues that are contributing to their current **maladaptive** behaviour.

# Psychological therapies

 Psychoanalysis

**Repression and the unconscious mind** – Many of the factors that cause behaviour operate at an unconscious level, and are the result of **repressed** memories or unresolved conflicts from childhood. During **psychoanalysis**, the therapist attempts to trace these influences to their origins and help the individual to deal with them.

**Free association** – The patient expresses thoughts exactly as they occur, even though they may appear unimportant to the individual. This is intended to reveal areas of conflict and to bring memories that have been repressed into consciousness. The therapist then helps to interpret these memories, and the individual may add further thoughts and feelings.

**Therapist interpretation** – The therapist draws tentative conclusions about the possible cause(s) of the problem. Patients may offer resistance to these conclusions (e.g. by changing the subject), or may display transference, where they recreate feelings associated with the problem and transfer these feelings onto the therapist.

**Working through** – Patient and therapist examine the same issues over and over again in an attempt to gain greater clarity concerning the causes of their problematic behaviour. b believed this was the process that produced the greatest changes in the patient, and distinguished psychoanalytic treatment from any other type of psychological therapy

 Strengths

**Effectiveness** – An analysis of 10,000 patient histories estimated that 80% benefitted from psychoanalysis compared to 60% who received therapies based on different approaches (**Bergin**). This provides modest support for the effectiveness of psychoanalysis as a treatment for **neurotic illnesses**.

**Length of treatment** – A study of 450 patients by **Tschuschke et al.** found that psychodynamic therapies, such as psychoanalysis, were more effective in the long-term. The longer the psychotherapeutic treatments took, the better the outcomes were, indicating that it takes motivation and effort from the patient for the treatment to be truly effective.

 Limitations

**No better than placebo** – A therapy is only as good as the underlying theory. **Eysenck** argued that '…the obvious failure of Freudian therapy to significantly improve on **spontaneous remission** or **placebo** treatment is the clearest proof we have of the inadequacy of Freudian theory'. Eysenck also points out that the success of **behavioural therapies** casts further doubts on the **validity** of psychoanalysis as a useful treatment.

**Appropriateness** – When developing psychoanalysis as a therapy, Freud failed to appreciate the differences between individuals in the way that modern psychotherapists do. The development of **humanistic therapies** addressed this problem by putting the client first, adjusting the therapy to suit the individual client rather than imposing specific theories on them.

**False memories** – Critics of psychoanalysis claim that some therapists are not helping patients to recover *repressed* memories, but are unwittingly planting **false memories** of sexual abuse or even alien abduction. All psychoanalysis assumes that a patient can reliably recall early memories that have been repressed, but as yet there is little evidence to support this.

Continued on next page

| Cognitive psychology: Memory | | Defining and explaining psychological abnormality | Biological therapies |
| Developmental psychology: Early social development | | | Psychological therapies 1 |
| Research methods | | **Treating abnormality** | **Psychological therapies 2** |
| Biological psychology: Stress | | | |
| Social psychology: Social influence | | | |
| **Individual differences: Psychotherapy (abnormality)** | | | |

## KEY TERMS

### REBT

- Rational-emotive behaviour therapy.
- A **CBT** that helps people change dysfunctional emotions and behaviours.
- It does this by making them aware of their self-defeating beliefs and replacing them with more constructive ones.

### Systematic desensitisation

- Based on **classical conditioning** (the **behavioural approach**).
- A therapy used to treat phobias and problems involving anxiety.
- A client is gradually exposed to the threatening situation under relaxed conditions until the anxiety reaction is extinguished.

---

**Step 1:** Patient is taught how to relax their muscles completely. (A relaxed state is incompatible with anxiety.)

**Step 2:** Therapist and patient together construct a desensitisation heierarchy – a series of imagined scenes, each one causing a little more anxiety than the previous one.

**Step 3:** Patient gradually works his/her way through desensitisation hierarchy, visualising each anxiety-evoking event while engaging in the competing relaxation response.

**Step 4:** Once the patient has mastered one step in the hierarchy (i.e. they can remain relaxed while imagining it), they are ready to move onto the next.

**Step 5:** Patient eventually masters the feared situation that caused them to seek help in the first place.

---

### ⟳ PUTTING IT ALL TOGETHER

Systematic desensitisation is derived from the behavioural approach and is based on the principles of classical conditioning. REBT is derived from the cognitive approach, and focuses on changing the irrational thoughts that determine **maladaptive** behaviour.

## Psychological therapies

###  Systematic desensitisation (SD)

**Systematic desensitisation** is used in the treatment of anxiety, particularly anxiety associated with **phobias**.

- Achieved by introducing feared object/situation *gradually*, working through a hierarchy of scenes, each causing more anxiety than the previous one.
- Individuals can overcome their anxieties by learning to relax in the presence of stimuli that had previously made them anxious.
- The two responses of relaxation and fear are incompatible and the fear is eventually dispelled.
- SD can also work without presenting the feared stimulus but having the client *imagine* it.

###  Strengths

**Appropriateness** – Behavioural therapies, such as SD, are relatively quick and require less effort on the patient's part than other psychotherapies. Patients are more likely to persevere, making treatment more likely to succeed.

**Effectiveness** – SD is successful for a range of anxiety disorders, such as fear of flying. **Capafóns** found that **aerophobics** had less anxiety after SD compared with a control group.

###  Limitations

**Symptom substitution** – SD may *appear* to resolve a problem, but simply eliminating symptoms (rather than dealing with the *cause* of **anxiety**) may result in other symptoms appearing later on.

**Not universally effective** – SD appears to be less effective in treating anxieties that have an underlying adaptive component (e.g. fear of dangerous animals) than those that are acquired as a result of personal experience.

###  Cognitive behavioural therapy (CBT)

**Cognitive behavioural therapies**, such as **REBT**, are based on the idea that many problems are the result of irrational thinking.

- REBT helps the patient understand this irrationality and the consequences of thinking in this way.
- Helps them to change any self-defeating thoughts and become happier and less anxious.
- During therapy, the patient is encouraged to dispute self-defeating beliefs.
- Achieved through *pragmatic* disputing (showing the lack of usefulness of existing beliefs).
- Person then moves to more rational interpretations of events.

###  Strengths

**Appropriateness** – A particular strength of REBT is that it's usefulness is not limited to people suffering from mental disorders, but is also useful for non-clinical populations (e.g. people suffering from examination anxiety).

**Effectiveness** – In a **meta-analysis** by **Engels et al.**, REBT was shown to be effective in the treatment of a number of different types of disorder, including **OCD** and **agoraphobia**.

###  Limitations

**Irrational environments** – REBT fails to address irrational environments that exist beyond the therapeutic situation (e.g. a bullying boss), which continue to produce and reinforce irrational thoughts and maladaptive behaviour.

**Not suitable for all** – REBT does not always work and is not always what people want. Some people fail to put the principles into practice and others do not want the 'direct' sort of advice of REBT.

# Glossary

**A-B-C model** Refers to the three components of experience that can be used to judge whether an individual's belief system is distorted. A (activating event) leads to B (belief) and ultimately C (consequences). (page 53)

**ACTH** *see* adrenocorticotrophic hormone.

**Adrenal cortex** A region of the adrenal gland, located above the kidneys. The adrenal cortex (outer region) manufactures glucocortoids (such as cortisol) and various sex hormones, such as testosterone. (page 30)

**Adrenal medulla** A region of the adrenal gland, located above the kidneys. The adrenal medulla (inner region) produces adrenaline and noradrenaline. (page 30)

**Adrenaline** A hormone associated with arousal of the autonomic nervous system (e.g. raised heart rate). It is also a neurotransmitter. Americans use the term 'epinephrine'. (pages 30, 38, 54)

**Adrenocorticotrophic hormone (ACTH)** A hormone produced in the pituitary gland as a response to stress. Its principal effect is the release of cortisol from the adrenal cortex. (page 30)

**Aerophobia** Fear of flying. (page 56)

**Agentic shift** People may move from being in a state where they take personal responsibility for their actions (an autonomous state) to a state where they believe they are acting on behalf of an authority figure (an agentic state). (page 44)

**Agentic state** A state where people believe they are acting on behalf of an authority figure. (page 44)

**Agoraphobia** Fear of being in places or situations from which escape might be difficult. (pages 52, 56)

**Aim** A statement of what the researcher(s) intend to find out in a research study. Often confused with hypothesis. (page 21)

**Animal experiment** An experiment using non-human animals, often conducted because of ethical issues involving the use of human participants. (page 11)

**ANS** *see* autonomic nervous system.

**Antigens** Molecules (such as bacteria, viruses, toxins) which invade the body and are targeted by the immune system. (page 31)

**Anti-Semitism** Hostility and prejudice against Jews. (page 44)

**Anticonformity** The refusal or failure to conform to the generally accepted standards, conventions or rules of a group. (page 45)

**Antipsychotics** Drugs that are effective in the treatment of psychotic illnesses, such as schizophrenia. (page 54)

**Anxiety** A nervous emotional state where we fear that something unpleasant is about to happen. People often become anxious when they are in stressful situations. Anxiety tends to be accompanied by physiological arousal (e.g. a pounding heart and rapid shallow breathing). (pages 7, 15, 32, 38, 52, 55, 56)

**Articulatory process** A component of the phonological loop which acts as an 'inner voice', i.e. words/sounds are verbally repeated. (page 5)

**Articulatory suppression task** An activity which prevents rehearsal of words in the articulatory loop. (page 5)

**Atherosclerosis** The thickening of walls of the arteries which may lead to a heart attack. (page 31)

**Attachment** An emotional bond between two people that endures over time. Leads to certain behaviours such as clinging and proximity-seeking. Serves the function of protecting an infant. (pages 11, 13, 14, 15, 16, 17, 18)

**Attachment disorder** A psychiatric disorder characterised by an individual's inability to identify a preferred attachment figure. (page 16)

**Attribution** When observing behaviour (our own or someone else's) we provide explanations for the behaviour. These explanations will be dispositional or situational. (page 46)

**Attributional style** A personality attribute that indicates how people consistently explain their experiences to themselves. (page 46)

**Attrition** The loss of participants from a study over time. This is likely to leave a biased sample or a sample that is too small. (page 25)

**Autonomic nervous system (ANS)** governs the body's involuntary activities (e.g. stress, heart beat) and is self-regulating (autonomous). It is divided into the sympathetic branch (fight or flight) and the parasympathetic branch (rest and digest). (pages 30, 31)

**Autonomous state** A state where people take personal responsibility for their actions. (page 44)

**Bar chart** The height of each bar represents the frequency of that item. The categories are placed on the horizontal ($x$ axis) and frequency is on the vertical ($y$ axis). Bar charts are suitable for words and numbers (nominal or ordinal/interval data). (page 26)

**BBs** *see* beta-blockers.

**Behaviour checklist** A systematic method for recording observations where a list of behaviourial categories is used. The observer(s) can note everytime any behaviour on the checklist is observed. (page 22)

**Behavioural approach to psycholopathology** Behaviourists believe that normal *and* abnormal behaviours are acquired as a result of experiences that we have in life. Abnormal behaviours are learned through the processes of conditioning and social learning. (pages 52, 55, 56)

**Behavioural categories** Dividing a target behaviour (such as attachment or sociability) into a subset of component behaviours to enable objective and reliable observations of the target behaviour. (pages 22, 23, 27)

**Benzodiazepines (BZs)** A group of drugs that have a tranquillising effect and are used to treat anxiety and stress. Work by slowing down the activity of the central nervous system. (page 38, 54)

**Beta-blockers (BBs)** A drug that decreases anxiety by blocking the action of adrenaline and noradrenaline during sympathetic arousal. (pages 38, 54)

**Biological approach to psychopathology** Explains behaviour in terms of physiological and/or genetic causes. A mental disorder represents the consequences of a malfunction of biological processes. (page 50)

**Brain scanning** A variety of techniques used to investigate brain functioning by taking images of a living brain. This makes it possible to match regions of the brain to behaviour by asking participants to engage in particular activities while the scan is taking place. (page 4)

**Buffer** Something (e.g. a physical barrier or an ideological justification) that protects an individual from perceiving the true impact of their actions. (pages 43, 44)

**BZs** *see* benzodiazepines.

**Capacity** A measure of how much can be held in memory. Measured in terms of bits of information such as number of digits. (page 4)

**Cardiovascular disorder** Disorders of the heart or circulatory system, including hypertension (high blood pressure, and heart disease). (pages 30, 34, 35, 38, 54)

**Case study** A research method that involves a detailed study of a single individual, institution or event. (pages 4, 5, 15, 16, 20, 51)

**CBT** *see* Cognitive behavioural therapy.

**Central executive** Monitors and coordinates all other mental functions in the working memory model. (page 5)

**Central nervous system (CNS)** Comprises the brain and the spinal cord. (page 38)

**CHD** *see* coronary heart disease.

**Chunking** Miller proposed that the capacity of STM can be enhanced by grouping sets of digits or letters into meaningful units or 'chunks'. (page 3)

**CI** *see* cognitive interview.

**Civil disobedience** A group's refusal to obey a law because they believe the law is immoral. (page 47)

**Classical conditioning** A new response (conditioned response, CR) is learned when a neutral stimulus (NS) is associated with an unconditioned stimulus (UCS). Initially, the UCS produced an unconditioned response (UCR). After learning, the NS becomes a conditioned stimulus (CS) which produces a CR. (pages 11, 52, 56)

**Clinical interview** A form of unstructured or semi-structured interview, where the interviewer may start with a few prepared questions but further questions develop in response to the answers provided by the interviewee. Similar to the interview conducted when you consult your doctor. (page 22)

**Closed question** Question that has a range of answers from which respondents select one; produces quantitative data. (pages 22, 27)

**Coding system** A systematic method for recording observations in which individual behaviours are given a code for ease of recording. (page 22)

**Cognitive approach to psychopathology** Psychopathological behaviour is explained in terms of irrational and negative thinking about the world. If this faulty thinking can be changed, the problem will disappear. (page 53)

**Cognitive behavioural therapy (CBT)** A combination of cognitive therapy (to change maladaptive thoughts and beliefs) and behavioural therapy (to change behaviour in response to these thoughts and beliefs). (pages 37, 56)

**Cognitive distortions** Dysfunctional thought processes. For example, processing information in a way likely to cause anxiety, or drawing faulty conclusions after processing information. (page 53)

**Cognitive interview (CI)** A police technique for interviewing witnesses to a crime based on what psychologists have found out about memory. (page 8)

**Cohort effects** One group of participants (cohort) may have unique characteristics because of time-specific experiences during their development, such as being a child during the Second World War. This may act as an extraneous variable. (page 28)

**Collectivist culture** Any culture which places more value on the 'collective' rather than the individual, and on interdependence rather than independence. The opposite is true of individualist culture. (pages 14, 40, 49)

**Compliance** Going along with others to gain their approval or avoid their disapproval. This is a result of social comparison, which enables an individual to adjust their behaviour to that of the group. There is no change in the person's underlying attitude, only their public behaviour. (pages 40, 41, 42)

**Conclusions** The implications drawn from a study: what the findings tell us about people in general rather than just about the particular participants in a study. (page 28)

**Concordance rates** A measure of similarity between two individuals or sets of individuals on a given trait, usually expressed as a percentage. (page 50)

**Concurrent validity** Establishing validity by comparing an existing method of measurement (e.g. test, questionnaire) with the one you are interested in. (page 23)

**Conditioned response (CR)** In classical conditioning, the response elicited by the conditioned stimulus i.e. a new association has been learned so that the neutral stimulus (NS) now produces the unconditioned response (UCR) which is now called the CR. (page 11)

**Conditioned stimulus (CS)** In classical conditioning, the neutral stimulus (NS) after it has been paired with the unconditioned stimulus. The NS now elicits the unconditioned response UCR, now called a conditioned response (CR). (page 11)

**Confederate** An individual in a study who is not a real participant and has been instructed how to behave by the investigator/experimenter. (pages 28, 40, 41, 43, 45, 47)

**Confidentiality** A participant's right to have personal information protected. The Data Protection Act makes confidentiality a legal right. (page 24)

**Conformity** A form of social influence that results from exposure to the majority position and leads to compliance with that position. It is the tendency for people to adopt the behaviour, attitudes and values of other members of the group. (pages 40, 45, 47)

**Content analysis** A kind of observational study in which behaviour is observed indirectly in written or verbal material such as interviews, conversations, books, diaries or TV programmes. (pages 20, 27)

**Continuity hypothesis** The view that there is a link between an infant's attachment relationship and later behaviour. (page 12)

**Control** The degree to which workers perceive that they have control over important aspects of their work, such as deadlines, procedures, etc. (page 34)

**Control condition/group** The condition (in a repeated measures design) or group (in an independent groups design) that provides a baseline measure of behaviour without the experimental treatment (IV), so that the effect of the experimental treatment may be assessed. (page 21)

**Controlled observation** A form of investigation in which behaviour is observed but under controlled conditions, as opposed to a naturalistic observation. (pages 11, 12, 13, 20, 22, 28)

**Coronary heart disease (CHD)** Failure of blood vessels to supply adequate blood to the heart. (page 35)

**Correlation coefficient** A number between −1 and +1 that tells us how closely the co-variables in a correlational analysis are related. (page 26)

**Correlation** The relationship between two variables. (pages 17, 26, 32)

**Correlational analysis** Determines the extent of a relationship between two co-variables. (pages 20, 26, 33, 34, 36, 47)

**Corticotrophin-releasing factor (CRF)** is a neurotransmitter involved in the stress response. It is released by the hypothalamus and triggers production of ACTH in the pituitary gland. (page 30)

**Cortisol** A hormone released by the adrenal glands that is produced when an animal is stressed. (pages 30, 31)

**Counterbalancing** An experimental technique used to overcome order effects. Counterbalancing ensures that each condition is tested first or second in equal amounts. (page 21)

**Co-variable** A variable in a correlation analysis that is believed to vary systematically with another co-variable. (page 20, 26)

**Covert observation** Observing people without their knowledge, e.g. using one-way mirrors. This is done because participants are likely to change their behaviour if they know they are being observed. (pages 22, 24)

**CR** see conditioned response.

**CRF** see corticotrophin-releasing factor.

**Cross-cultural study** A kind of natural experiment in which the IV is different cultural practices and the DV is a behaviour such as attachment. This enables researchers to investigate the effects of culture/socialisation. (pages 12, 28)

**Cross-sectional study** One group of participants of a young age are compared with another, older group of participants, with a view to finding out the influence of age on the behaviour in question. (page 28)

**CS** see conditioned stimulus.

**Cultural relativism** The view that ideas of normal and abnormal behaviour differ from culture to culture. (page 49)

**Culture** The rules, customs, morals and ways of interacting that bind together members of a society or some other collection of people. (page 14)

**Daily hassles** Those frustrating, irritating everyday experiences that occur regularly in our work, home and personal life. (pages 32, 33)

**Daily uplifts** The minor positive experiences of everyday life that often counter the negative effects of daily hassles. (page 33)

**Day care** A form of temporary care (i.e. not all day and night) not provided by parents. Usually takes place outside the home and includes childminding and day nurseries. (pages 15, 17, 18)

**Debriefing** A post-research interview designed to inform participants about the true nature of a study, and to restore them to the state they were in at the start of the study. It may also be used to gain feedback about the procedures used in the study. (page 24)

**Decay** An explanation for forgetting where the memory trace in our brain disintegrates over time. (pages 2, 4)

**Deception** This occurs when a participant is not told the true aims of a study (e.g. what participation will involve). Thus the participants cannot give truly informed consent. (pages 24, 43)

**Demand characteristics** A cue that makes participants aware of what the researcher expects to find or how participants are expected to behave. (pages 6, 20, 21)

**Dependent variable (DV)** Depends in some way on the independent variable (IV). The DV is measured to assess the effects of the IV. (pages 20, 21, 28)

**Depression** A mental disorder characterised by a lowering of mood, often accompanied by difficulty thinking, concentrating and sleeping, as well as feelings of anxiety. (pages 15, 32, 33, 46, 49, 50, 51, 52, 53, 54)

**Deprivation dwarfism** Children who experience emotional deprivation are often physically smaller. Emotional disturbance (stress) may affect the production of hormones, such as growth hormones, and lead to a kind of physical 'dwarfism'. (page 16)

**Deviation from ideal mental health** Abnormality is seen as deviating from an ideal of positive mental health. This includes a positive attitude toward the self and an accurate perception of reality. (page 49)

**Deviation from social norms** Abnormal behaviour is a deviation from unwritten rules about how one 'ought' to behave. Violation of these rules is considered abnormal. (page 49)

**Diary method** A method of investigating behaviour where participants keep a regular record of their experiences, thoughts and behaviour. (page 33)

**Diathesis-stress model** In the case of certain disorders, individuals inherit a vulnerability for the disorder (diathesis) which develops only if such individuals are exposed to difficult environmental conditions (stress). The greater the underlying vulnerability, the less stress is needed to trigger the disorder. (page 50)

**Differential experience hypothesis** The ability to distinguish between groups of people improves as contact with those groups increases. (page 7)

**Digit span technique** A technique to assess the span of immediate (short-term) memory. Participants are given progressively more digits in a list to see how many can be recalled. (page 3)

**Directional hypothesis** States the direction of the predicted difference between two conditions or two groups of participants. (page 21)

**Disinhibited attachment** A type of insecure attachment where children do not discriminate about people they choose as attachment figures. Such children will treat near-strangers with inappropriate familiarity (overfriendliness) and may be attention-seeking. (pages 13, 16)

**Displacement** An explanation for forgetting, where existing information is displaced out of memory by new information. (pages 2, 4)

**Dispositional** Accounting for an individual's behaviour in terms of their personality or disposition. (page 46)

**Dopamine** A neurotransmitter involved in the sensation of pleasure, unusually high levels are associated with schizophrenia. (page 54)

**Double blind technique** Neither the participant or investigator are aware of the research aims or other important details of a study, and thus have no expectations that might alter the participant's behaviour. (page 21)

**Duration** A measure of how long a memory lasts before it is no longer available. (pages 2, 8)

**DV** see dependent variable.

**Ecological validity** A form of external validity; the ability to generalise a research effect beyond the particular setting in which it is demonstrated, to other settings. (pages 2, 20, 23)

**ECT (electro-convulsive shock therapy)** The administration of an electrical current through electrodes on the scalp. This induces a seizure, which can be effective in relieving major depression. (page 54)

**Ego** The conscious, rational part of the personality. It develops because a young child must deal with the constraints of reality and so is governed by the reality principle. (page 51)

**Ego defences** Unconscious methods, such as repression and projection, which help protect the individual from feelings of anxiety. (page 51)

**Emotion-focused coping** The use of strategies that deal only with the emotional distress associated with stressful events. (page 36)

**Encoding** The way information is changed so it can be stored in memory. Information enters the brain via the senses (e.g. eyes and ears) and is then stored (encoded) in various forms, such as visual codes (like a picture), acoustic forms (sounds), or a semantic form (the meaning of the experience). (pages 2, 8)

**Episodic buffer** In the working memory model, a store that receives input from many sources, temporarily stores this information, then integrates it in order to construct a mental episode of what is being experienced right now. (page 5)

**Ethical committee** (also called institutional review board IRB). A group of people within a research institution that must approve a study before it begins. (page 24)

**Ethical guidelines** Concrete, quasi-legal documents that help to guide conduct within psychology. (page 24)

**Ethical issues** arise in research where there are conflicting sets of values concerning the goals, procedures or outcomes of a research study. (pages 22, 24, 55)

**EV** see extraneous variable.

**EWT** see eyewitness testimony.

**Event sampling** An observational technique: counting the number of times a certain behaviour (event) occurs. (page 22)

**Experiment** A research method to investigate causal relationships by observing the effect of an independent variable on the dependent variable (see lab, field and natural experiment). (pages 20, 21, 23, 28, 38, 58)

**Experimental condition/group** In a repeated measures design, the condition containing the independent variable, or in an independent groups design, the group of participants who receive the experimental treatment (the IV). (page 21)

**Experimental realism** The extent to which participants become involved in an experiment and become less influenced by cues about how to behave. (page 23)

**Experimenter bias** *see* investigator bias.

**Experimenter effect** *see* investigator effect.

**External reliability** Concerns consistency *over time* such that it is possible to obtain the same results on subsequent occasions when a measure is used. (page 23)

**External validity** Concerns the degree to which a research finding can be generalised to, for example, other settings (ecological validity), or other groups of people (population validity), and over time (historical validity). (pages 23, 43)

**Externals (external control)** Individuals who tend to believe that their behaviour and experience is caused by events outside their own control. (page 46)

**Extraneous variable (EV)** Any variable, other than the IV, which may potentially affect the DV and thereby confound the findings. Order effects, participant variables and situational variables may act as EVs. (pages 20, 21, 23)

**Eyewitness testimony (EWT)** The evidence provided in court by a person who witnessed a crime, with a view to identifying the perpetrator of the crime. The accuracy of eyewitness recall may be affected during initial encoding, subsequent storage and/or eventual retrieval. (pages 6, 7)

**Failure to function adequately** Mentally healthy people are judged as being able to operate within certain acceptable limits. If abnormal behaviour interferes with daily functioning, it may be considered abnormal. (page 49)

**False consensus effect** The belief that the majority of people share similar beliefs to oneself. (page 41)

**False memories** Remembering events, especially traumatic events that have not actually occurred. May be prompted by the suggestion of a therapist. (page 55)

**Field experiment** A controlled experiment that is conducted outside a laboratory (i.e. not in a specially designed environment). The experimenter goes to the participant rather than vice versa. The IV is still manipulated by the experimenter, and therefore causal relationships can be demonstrated. (page 20)

**Flight or flight** A term meaning an animal is energised to either fight or run away in response to a sudden (acute) stressor. (page 30)

**GABA (Gamma-amino-butyric-acid)** A neurotransmitter that regulates excitement in the nervous system, thus acting as a natural form of anxiety reducer. (page 38)

**Genetic inheritance** The reception of genetically coded traits as a result of transmission from parent to offspring. (pages 50, 55)

**Hardiness training** The aim of hardiness training is to acquire the characteristics of a 'hardy' personality; to increase self-confidence and a sense of self-control within an individual's life. (page 37)

**Hardy personality** A type of personality, which provides a defence against the negative effects of stress. A person with hardy personality is high in control, commitment and challenge. (pages 35, 37)

**Hawthorne effect** The tendency for participants to alter their behaviour merely as a result of knowing that they are being observed. (page 28)

**Heroic imagination** A mental orientation that involves imagining facing potentially risky situations (e.g. pressure to conform to an antisocial behaviour), struggling with the hypothetical problems these situations raise, and considering one's likely actions and their consequences. (page 45)

**Hippocampus** A structure in the subcortical (i.e. 'under' the cortex) area of each hemisphere of the forebrain, associated with memory. Part of the limbic system, therefore involved in motivation, emotion and learning. (page 4)

**Historical validity** A form of external validity; the ability to generalise a research effect beyond the particular historical period in which it was demonstrated, to other historical periods. (page 23)

**Holocaust** The systematic, bureaucratic, state-sponsored persecution and murder of approximately six million Jews by the Nazi regime and its collaborators. 'Holocaust' is a word of Greek origin meaning 'sacrifice by fire'. (pages 44, 47)

**Hormones** Chemical substances that circulate in the blood and only affect target organs. They are produced in large quantities but disappear very quickly. Their effects are slow in comparison to the nervous system, but very powerful. (page 16)

**Humanistic therapies** Methods of treatment for mental disorder that focus on the present and aim to enhance the client's self-esteem so that the client can take control and recover. (page 55)

**Hypothalamus** A structure in the subcortical (i.e. 'under' the cortex) area of each hemisphere of the forebrain. It functions to regulate bodily temperature, metabolic processes such as eating, and other autonomic activities, including emotional responses. (page 30)

**Hypothesis** A precise and testable statement about the assumed relationship between variables. (page 21)

**Id** The irrational, primitive part of the personality. It demands immediate satisfaction and is ruled by the pleasure principle. (page 51)

**Identification** Adopting the attitudes and behaviours of others. Thus an individual feels more a part of the group, and is more likely to be accepted by them. (pages 40, 41)

**Immune system** Designed to defend the body against antigens (bacteria, viruses, toxins, etc.) that would otherwise invade it. White blood cells (leucocytes) identify and eliminate foreign bodies (antigens). (pages 30, 31, 34)

**Imposed etic** A technique or theory that is developed in one culture and then used to study people in a different culture. Such a technique or theory may be meaningless when used with people who have had different experiences or have different values. (page 14)

**Independence/independent behaviour** Behaving in a way that shows freedom from any control or influence of other group members. (pages 40, 45, 46)

**Independent groups design** An experimental design where participants are allocated to two (or more) groups, each one receiving a different treatment. (page 21)

**Independent variable (IV)** An event that is directly manipulated by the experimenter in order to observe its effects on the dependent variable (DV). (pages 20, 21, 28)

**Individualist culture** A culture that values independence rather than reliance on others, in contrast to many non-Western cultures that could be described as collectivist. (pages 14, 40, 49)

**Informational social influence** The result of wanting to be right, i.e. looking to others for the right answer, and conforming to their opinion. (page 42)

**Informed consent** In terms of ethics, participants must be given comprehensive information concerning the nature and purpose of a study and their role in it. This is necessary in order that they can make an informed decision about whether to participate. (pages 24, 43)

**Inner scribe** In the working memory model, a component of the visuo-spatial sketchpad which deals with spatial relations, such as the arrangement of objects in the visual field. (page 5)

**Insecure attachment** Develops as a result of caregiver's lack of sensitive responding to the infant's needs. May be associated with poor cognitive and emotional development. (page 13, 14, 17)

**Insecure-avoidant attachment** Infants who are willing to explore and are unresponsive to mother's return; they generally avoid social interaction and intimacy with others. (pages 13, 14)

**Insecure-disorganised attachment** Infants who lack consistent patterns of attachment behaviour. (page 13)

**Insecure-resistant (ambivalent) attachment** Infants are less interested in exploring and show distress on mother's return; generally they both seek and reject intimacy and social interaction. (pages 13, 14)

**Institutional care** An 'institution' is a place dedicated to a particular task, such as looking after children awaiting adoption, caring for the mentally ill or looking after patients in hospital. It is a place where people are looked after for a period of time, as opposed to day care or outpatient care where people go home every day. In the past, such institutions had fairly strict regimes and offered little emotional care. (page 15)

**Inter-interviewer reliability** The extent to which there is agreement between two or more interviewers in the answers they elicit from interviewees. (pages 20, 23)

**Inter-observer reliability** The extent to which there is agreement between two or more raters involved in rating a behaviour. (pages 20, 23, 27)

**Internal reliability** concerns consistency *within* a set of scores or items. (page 23)

**Internal validity** concerns whether a study or measurement has tested what it set out to test. (pages 2, 23, 43)

**Internal working model** A cluster of concepts about relationships. In the short-term, it gives a child insight into their caregiver's behaviour. In the long term, it acts as a template for future relationships because it generates expectations about how people behave. (page 12)

**Internalisation** Going along with others because of an acceptance of their point of view. This is a result of an examination of the group's position, which may lead to *validation* of the person's own views, or acceptance of the group's views both in public and in private. (pages 40, 41, 42, 47)

**Internals (internal control)** Individuals who tend to believe that they are responsible for their behaviour and experience (as distinct from external influences) (page 46)

**Interval data** are measured using units of equal intervals, such as when counting correct answers or using any 'public' unit of measurement. (page 26)

**Intervening variable** A variable that comes between two other variables that is used to explain the relationship between those two variables. (page 28)

**Interview** A research method or technique that involves a face-to-face, 'real-time' interaction with another individual and results in the collection of data. (pages 20, 22, 23, 28, 34)

**Interviewer bias** The effect of an interviewer's expectations on a respondent's behaviour. Such expectations are communicated unconsciously. (pages 20, 23)

**Investigator effect** Anything that the investigator/experimenter does that has an effect on a participant's performance in a study, other than what was intended. (pages 20, 21, 28)

**Investigator/experimenter bias** The effect that an investigator/experimenter's expectations has on the participants and thus on the results of a research study. (page 28)

**IV** *see* independent variable.

**Lab experiment** An experiment carried out in a controlled setting. Lab experiments tend to demonstrate high experimental (internal) validity and low ecological (external) validity, though this isn't always true. (pages 2, 3, 4, 5, 6, 7, 8, 9, 11, 20, 31, 40, 41, 43)

**Leading (misleading) question** A question that, either by its form or content, suggests to the witness what answer is desired or leads him to the desired answer. (pages 6, 20, 22)

**Learning theory** The name given to a group of explanations i.e. classical and operant conditioning. Essentially, these explain behaviour in terms of learning rather than any inborn tendencies (the biological/evolutionary approach) or higher order thinking (the cognitive approach). (page 11)

**Leucocytes** are white blood cells, the cells of the immune system that defend the body against infectious disease and foreign bodies. (page 31)

**Levels of measurement** The different ways of measuring something; the lower levels are less precise. (page 26)

**Life changes** Events (e.g. divorce or bereavement) that require a significant adjustment in a person's life, thus they are a significant source of stress. (pages 32, 33)

**Locus of control** An aspect of our personality: people differ in their beliefs about whether the outcomes of their actions are contingent on what they do (internal control) or on events outside their personal control (external control). (page 46)

**Long-term memory (LTM)** Memory for events that have happened in the past. Lasts anywhere from 2 minutes to 100 years and has potentially unlimited duration and capacity. (pages 2, 4)

**Longitudinal study** Observation of the same items over a long period of time. (pages 12, 16, 17, 28, 34)

**LTM** *see* long-term memory.

**Majority influence** A form of social influence where people follow the norm established by the majority. (pages 40, 41, 45, 47)

**Maladaptive behaviour** Behaviours that inhibit a person's ability to cope with, or adjust to, particular situations. (pages 30, 36, 46, 49, 52, 53, 55, 56)

**Matched pairs design** An experimental design where pairs of participants are matched in terms of key variables such as age and IQ. One member of each pair is placed in the experimental group and the other member in the control group. (page 21)

**Mean** Calculated by adding up all the numbers and dividing by the number of numbers. It can only be used with interval or ratio data. (pages 26, 27)

**Measures of central tendency** A descriptive statistic that provides information about a 'typical' number for a data set. (page 26)

**Measures of dispersion** A descriptive statistic that provides information about how spread out a set of scores are. (page 26)

**Median** The middle value in an ordered list, suitable for ordinal or interval data. (page 26)

**Meta-analysis** A researcher looks at the findings from a number of different studies in order to reach a general conclusion about a particular hypothesis. (pages 7, 8, 14, 17, 28, 31, 35, 38, 40, 41, 46, 56)

**Minority influence** A form of social influence where people reject the established norm of the majority of group members and move to the position of the minority. (pages 41, 47)

**Mnemonic techniques** Methods used to improve your memory for things. (page 9)

**Mode** The value that is most common. (page 26)

**Monocausal emphasis** Relying on just one causal factor when explaining an event. (page 44)

**Monotropy** The idea that the one relationship that the infant has with his/her primary attachment figure is of special significance in emotional development. (page 12)

**Multi-store model (MSM)** An explanation of memory based on three separate memory stores, and how information is transferred between these stores. (page 4)

**Mundane realism** Refers to how a study mirrors the real world. The experimental environment is realistic to the degree to which experiences encountered in the experimental environment will occur in everyday life (the 'real world'). (pages 20, 23)

**Natural experiment** A research method in which the experimenter cannot manipulate the independent variable directly, but where it varies naturally, and the effect on a dependent variable can be observed. (pages 2, 7, 16, 20, 28, 31, 32, 35, 36)

**Naturalistic observation** A research method carried out in a naturalistic setting, in which the investigator does not interfere in any way, but merely observes the behaviour(s) in question (likely to involve the use of structured observations). (pages 13, 15, 20, 22, 23)

**Negative correlation** As one co-variable increases, the other decreases. (page 26)

**Neuroanatomy** The branch of anatomy that deals with the structure of the brain and other parts of the nervous system. (page 50)

**Neurochemistry** The action of chemicals (e.g. neurotransmitters) in the brain and the drugs that influence neural activity. (page 50)

**Neuron** A specialised cell in the nervous system for transmission of information. (page 38)

**Neurotic illness** Describes a nonpsychotic mental illness that triggers feelings of distress and anxiety and impairs functioning. (page 55)

**Neurotransmitter** Chemical substances, such as serotonin or dopamine, which play an important part in the workings of the nervous system by transmitting nerve impulses across a synapse. (pages 38, 50, 54)

**Neutral stimulus (NS)** In classical conditioning, the stimulus that initially does not produce the target response i.e. it is neutral. Through association with the unconditioned stimulus (UCS), the NS acquires the properties of the UCS and becomes a conditioned stimulus (CS) producing a conditioned response (CR). (page 11)

**Nominal data** In separate categories, such as grouping people according to their favourite football team. (page 26)

**Non-directional hypothesis** Predicting that there will be a difference between two conditions or two groups of participants, without stating the direction of the difference. (page 21)

**Non-participant observation** An observational study where the observer is not taking part in the activity being observed. (page 22)

**Nonpsychotic illness** A psychotic illness is one where a patient loses touch with reality, such as schizophrenia. Neurotic illnesses are nonpsychotic. (page 55)

**Nonsense trigram** A group of three letters that have no meaning. (page 2)

**Noradrenaline** A hormone associated with arousal of the autonomic nervous system (e.g. raised heart rate), and also a neurotransmitter. (pages 30, 38, 54)

**Normative social influence** The result of wanting to be liked and be accepted as part of a group by following its norms. (page 42)

**NS** *see* neutral stimulus.

**Obedience alibi** Reaching a conclusion that obedience had a key role in Holocaust events when such a conclusion is unjustified given an analysis of the historical record. (page 44)

**Obedience to authority** A type of social influence whereby somebody acts in response to a direct order from a figure with perceived authority. There is also the implication that the person receiving the order is made to respond in a way that they would not have done without the order. (pages 43, 44, 45, 47)

**Observation/Observational techniques** The application of systematic methods of observation in an observational study, experiment (to measure the DV) or other study. (pages 20, 22, 23, 27, 28)

**Observational learning** Learning through observing others and imitating their behavior. (page 52)

**Observer bias** The tendency for observations to be influenced by expectations or prejudices. (pages 20, 23)

**Obsessive-compulsive disorder (OCD)** A mental disorder where anxiety arises from both obsessions (persistent and intrusive thoughts) and compulsions (means of controlling these thoughts). (pages 52, 56)

**OCD** *see* obsessive-compulsive disorder.

**Oedipal conflict** Incestuous feelings that a young boy develops for his mother, coupled with rivalry with the father for her affections, leading to castration anxiety. Resolution of this conflict leads to the development of the superego. (page 51)

**Open questions** A question that invites respondents to provide their own answers rather than to select an answer that has been provided. Tends to produce qualitative data. (page 22)

**Operant conditioning** Involves reinforcement each time you do something and it results in a pleasant consequence, the behaviour is 'stamped in' (reinforcement). It becomes more probable that you will repeat that behaviour in the future. If you do something and it results in an unpleasant consequence (punishment), it becomes less likely that you will repeat that behaviour. (pages 11, 52)

**Operationalise** Providing variables in a form that can be easily tested, i.e. the constituent operations are identified. (pages 21, 22)

**Opportunity sample** A sample of participants produced by selecting people who are most easily available at the time of the study. (page 25)

**Order effects** In a repeated measures design, an extraneous variable arising from the order in which conditions are presented. For example, participants do better the second time because they have had some practice. (page 21)

**Ordinal data** Ordered in some way, for example asking people to put a list of football teams in order of liking. The 'difference' between each item is not the same, i.e. the individual may like the first item a lot more than the second, but there might only be a small difference between the items ranked second and third. (page 26)

**Overt observation** An observational technique where observations are 'open', i.e. the participants are aware that they are being observed. (page 22)

**Own-age bias** The tendency to recognise or remember things more easily if they relate to your own age group. (page 7)

**Participant effects** A general term used to acknowledge the fact that participants react to cues in an experimental situation and that this may affect the validity of any conclusions drawn from the investigation. (pages 20, 28)

**Participant observation** A kind of observational study where the observer is also a participant in the activity being observed. This may affect the objectivity of their observations. (page 22)

**Participant variables** Characteristics of individual participants (such as age, intelligence, etc.) that might influence the outcome of a study. (page 21)

**Personal Views Survey** A measure of 'hardiness'. The overall hardiness score is a composite of three subscales: commitment, control, and challenge. (page 35)

**Phobia** A mental disorder characterised by high levels of anxiety that, when experienced, interfere with normal living. Includes specific and social phobias. (pages 52, 56)

**Phonological loop** A component of the working memory model that encodes speech sounds, involving maintenance rehearsal (repeating the words over and over, i.e. a *loop*). It is divided into a phonological store (inner ear) and an articulatory process (inner voice). (page 5)

**Phonological store** A component of the phonological loop which acts as an 'inner ear', i.e. storing sounds. (page 5)

**Pilot study** A small-scale trial of a study. Run to test any aspects of the design, with a view to making improvements. (page 22)

**Pituitary-adrenal system** Stress response involving the pituitary gland and adrenal medulla. It helps the body cope with chronic stressors. (pages 30, 31)

**Pituitary gland** Known as the 'master gland', the pituitary releases a variety of hormones that act on other glands throughout the body. (page 30)

**Placebo** A drug or treatment that contains no active ingredient or therapeutic procedure. (pages 38, 50, 54, 55)

**Pleasure principle** In Freudian psychology, the id's primitive desire to seek instant gratification and avoid pain at all costs. (page 51)

**Population validity** A form of external validity; the ability to generalise a research effect beyond the particular population from which the sample was drawn, to other populations. (page 23)

**Positive correlation** Co-variables increase together. (pages 17, 26)

**Post-event information** In eyewitness testimony, information supplied after the event, such as a leading question. (page 6)

**Predictive validity** A means of establishing validity by considering the extent to which the current measure predicts (or correlates with) other measures of the same construct measured at some time in the future. (page 13)

**Prefrontal cortex** The anterior part of the frontal lobe, involved in 'executive functions', such as complex cognitive behaviours, moderating socially-appropriate behaviours, personality and goal-directed behaviour (motivation). (page 4)

**Presumptive consent** A method of dealing with lack of informed consent or deception by asking a group of people who are similar to the participants whether they would agree to take part in a study. If this group of people consent to the procedures in the proposed study, it is *presumed* that the real participants would agree as well. (page 24)

**Primacy effect** The tendency to remember words from the start of a list. (page 4)

**Primary attachment figure** The person who has formed the closest bond with a child. Demonstrated by the intensity of the relationship. Usually a child's biological mother, but could be an adoptive mother, a father, grandmother, etc. (pages 12, 14, 15)

**Primary reinforcer** An innate reinforcer. (page 11)

**Privacy** A person's right to control the flow of information about themselves. If privacy is invaded, confidentiality should be protected. (page 24)

**Privation** The failure to develop any attachments during early life. This is contrasted with 'deprivation' or 'disruption' where attachment bonds have formed, but may be disrupted either through physical or simply emotional separation. Such disruption may last for weeks or a lifetime (in the case of parental death). (page 16)

**Problem-focused coping** The use of strategies designed directly to deal the stressful situation itself. (page 36)

**Projection** A form of ego defence whereby a person, unknowingly, displaces unacceptable feelings on to someone or something else as a means of coping. (page 51)

**Protection from harm** During a research study, participants should not experience negative physical effects, such as physical injury. Nor psychological effects, such as lowered self esteem or embarrassment. (pages 24, 43)

**Psychoanalysis** A therapy developed by Sigmund Freud to make the unconscious conscious and deal with the causes of abnormal behaviour. (page 55)

**Psychodynamic approach to psychopathology** Any approach that emphasises the dynamics of behaviour. In other words, what *drives* us to behave in particular ways. (page 51)

**Punishment** In operant conditioning, the application of an unpleasant stimulus such that the likelihood of the behaviour that led to it reoccurring is decreased. (page 11)

**Qualitative data** Expresses 'quality'. This includes descriptions, meanings, pictures and so on. The data cannot be counted or quantified but they can be turned into quantitative data by placing information in categories and counting instances. (pages 22, 27)

**Qualitative data analysis** Summarising qualitative data, for example by identifying themes and interpreting the meaning of an experience to the individual(s) concerned. (page 27)

**Quantitative data analysis** Any means of representing trends from numerical data, such as measures of central tendency. (page 26)

**Quantitative data** Represents how much or how long, or how many, etc. there are of something. Data that are measured in numbers or quantities. (pages 22, 26, 27)

**Quasi-experiments** Studies that are 'almost' experiments but lack one or more features of a true experiment, such as full experimenter control over the IV and random allocation of participants to conditions. This means that such studies cannot claim to demonstrate causal relationships. (pages 7, 28)

**Questionnaire** Data is collected through the use of written questions. (pages 7, 20, 22, 23, 31, 32, 34, 46)

**Quota sample** Groups of participants are selected according to their frequency in the population. Selection is done from each group using opportunity sampling. (page 25)

**Random allocation** Allocating participants to experimental groups using random techniques. (pages 21, 28)

**Random sample** A sample of participants produced by using a random technique. (page 25)

**Random technique** Method of selection that ensures each member of the population has an equal chance of being selected. For example, placing all names in a hat and drawing out the required number, or by assigning each person a number and using a random number table. (page 25)

**Range** The difference between the highest and lowest score in a data set. (pages 26, 27)

**Ratio data** A level of measurement where there is a true zero point, as in most measures of physical quantities. (page 26)

**Reality principle** In psychoanalytic theory, the drive by the ego to accommodate to the demands of the environment in a realistic way. (page 51)

**REBT** (Rational emotive behaviour therapy) A cognitive behavioural therapy that helps people change dysfunctional emotions and behaviours. It does this by making them aware of their self-defeating beliefs and replacing them with more constructive ones. (page 56)

**Recency effect** The tendency to remember words from the end of a list. (page 4)

**Regression** A form of ego defence whereby a person returns psychologically to an earlier stage of development rather than handling unacceptable impulses in a more adult way. Anxiety-provoking thoughts can thus be temporarily pushed into the unconscious. Often confused with repression. (page 51)

**Reinforcement** If a behaviour results in a pleasant state of affairs, the behaviour is 'stamped in' or reinforced. It then is more probable that the behaviour will be repeated in the future. Can be positive or negative reinforcement – both lead to an increased likelihood that the behaviour will be repeated. (page 11)

• **Reinforcer** Anything that provides reinforcement. (page 11)

**Reliability** A measure of consistency. (pages 23, 32)

**Repeated measure design** An experimental design where each participant takes part in every condition under test. (page 21)

**Repression** A form of ego defence whereby anxiety-provoking material is kept out of conscious awareness as a means of coping. (pages 51, 55)

**Right to withdraw** Participants should have the right to withdraw from participating in a study if they are uncomfortable in any way. They should also have the right to refuse permission for the researcher to use any data they produced. (page 24)

**Role conflict** This occurs when experiences at work interfere with family life and vice versa, e.g. an employee who always takes work home, or someone whose work performance is affected by their home life. (page 34)

**Role play** A controlled observation in which participants are asked to imagine how they would behave in certain situations, and then asked to act out the part. This method has the advantage of permitting the study of behaviours that might be unethical or difficult to find in the real world. (page 28)

**Sampling** The process of taking a sample. Any sampling technique aims to produce a representative selection of the target population. (pages 22, 23, 25, 27)

**Scattergram** A graphical representation of the relationship (i.e. the correlation) between two sets of scores. (page 26)

**Schizophrenia** A mental disorder where an individual has lost touch with reality and may experience symptoms such as delusions, hallucinations, grossly disorganised behaviour and flattened emotions. (pages 50, 53, 54)

**Scientific method** The method used in scientific research where scientists start by observing natural phenomena and then develop explanations and hypotheses that are tested using systematic research methods. (page 28)

**Secondary attachment figure** Acts as a kind of emotional safety net, and is therefore important in emotional development. Also contributes to social development. (page 12)

**Secondary reinforcer** A reinforcer that is acquired through experience. (page 11)

**Secure attachment** An infant who is willing to explore, easy to soothe and displays high stranger anxiety. The infant is comfortable with social interaction and intimacy. Such attachments are related to healthy subsequent cognitive and emotional development. Develops as a result of sensitive responding by attachment figure to the infant's needs. (pages 13, 14, 15, 16)

**Self-actualisation** A person's motivation to maximise their achievements and fulfil their potential. (page 49)

**Self-report technique** A research method that relies on the participant answering questions – either verbally (in an interview) or in writing (in a questionnaire). (pages 20, 23)

**Sensitive period** A biologically-determined period of time during which a child is particularly sensitive to a specific form of stimulation, resulting in the development of a specific response or characteristic. (pages 12, 16)

**Sensory memory** Information at the senses – information collected by your eyes, ears, nose, fingers and so on. Information is retained for a very brief period by the sensory registers (less than half a second). Capacity of sensory memory is very large. The method of encoding depends on the sense organ involved, i.e. visual for the eyes, acoustic for the ears. (page 4)

**Separation anxiety** Distress shown by an infant when separated from his/her attachment figure. (page 13)

**Serial position effect** Information is recalled better from the most recently presented material (the recency effect) or from the first information presented (the primacy effect). (page 4)

**Serotonin** A neurotransmitter found in the central nervous system. Low levels have been linked to many different behaviours and physiological processes, including aggression, eating disorders and depression. (pages 38, 50, 54)

**Short-term memory (STM)** Memory for immediate events. Lasts for a very short time and disappears unless rehearsed. Limited duration and limited capacity. Sometimes referred to as working memory. (pages 2, 3, 4)

**Single blind technique** A type of research design in which the participant is not aware of the research aims or of which condition of the experiment they are receiving. (page 21)

**Situational** Accounting for an individual's behaviour in terms of aspects of the environment or external factors, such as another person's behaviour or luck. (page 46)

**Situational variables** Any factor in the environment that could affect the dependent variable, such as noise, time of day or the behaviour of an investigator. (page 21)

**SM** see sensory memory.

**SNS** see sympathetic nervous system.

**STM** see short term memory.

**Social change** Occurs when a society as a whole adopts a new belief or way of behaving, which then becomes widely accepted as the norm. (page 47)

**Social desirability bias** The tendency for respondents to answer questions in a way that presents them in a better light. (pages 20, 23)

**Social heroism** Putting oneself at risk in the pursuit of an important principle. (page 45)

**Social impact theory** States that the likelihood that a person will respond to social influence will increase with *strength* (how important the influencing group is to the individual), *immediacy* (how close it is) and *number* (how many members it has). (page 42)

**Social learning theory** The assumption that people learn through indirect as well as direct rewards, by observing the behaviour of models (observational learning) and imitating such behaviour if others have been rewarded for such behaviour (vicarious reinforcement). (page 52)

**Social releasers** A social behaviour or characteristic that elicits a caregiving reaction. (page 12)

**Split-half method** A method of assessing internal reliability by comparing two halves of, for example, a psychological test to see if both halves produce a similar same score. (page 23)

**Spontaneous remission** The disappearance of psychopathological symptoms over time without formal treatment. (page 55)

**SRRS (Social Readjustment Rating Scale)** Developed by Holmes and Rahe to be able to test the idea that life changes are related to stress-related illnesses, such as anxiety and depression. (pages 32, 35)

**SSRIs (Social Readjustment Rating Scale)** Selective serotonin re-uptake inhibitors, a class of drug used in the treatment of depression. (page 54)

**Standard deviation** Shows the amount of variation in a data set. It assesses the spread of the data around the mean. (page 26)

**Standard interview** An interview that lacks the four CI components. (page 8)

**Standardised instructions** The instructions given to participants to tell them how to perform a task. (page 28)

**Standardised procedures** A set of procedures that are the same for all participants in order to be able to repeat a study. This includes standardised instructions. (page 28)

**STM** see short-term memory.

**Strange situation** Method to assess strength of attachment, conducted in a novel environment and involving eight episodes. An infant's behaviour is observed when mother leaves and returns, and when with a stranger. Measures attachment in terms of stranger anxiety and separation anxiety. (pages 13, 14)

**Stranger anxiety** Distress shown by an infant when approached by an unfamiliar person. (page 13)

**Stratified sample** Groups of participants are selected according to their frequency in the population. Selection is done randomly from each strata. (page 25)

**Stress** Experienced when the perceived demands of a situation are greater than the perceived ability to cope. (pages 30, 31, 32, 33, 34, 35, 36, 37, 38, 50)

**Stress inoculation training (SIT)** A type of CBT which trains people to cope with stressful situations more effectively by learning skills to protect them from the damaging effects of future stressors. (page 37)

**Structured interview** Any interview in which the questions are decided in advance. (pages 22, 35)

**Structured observation** An observer uses various 'systems' to organise observations, such as behavioural categories and sampling procedures. (page 22)

**Studies using a correlational analysis** see correlational analysis.

**Superego** This develops between the ages of three and six. It embodies the conscience and our sense of right and wrong, as well as notions of the ideal self. (page 51)

**Sympathetic arousal/branch/nervous system (SNS)** The part of the autonomic nervous system that is associated with physiological arousal and 'fight or flight' responses. (pages 30, 31, 54)

**Sympathomedullary pathway** A stress response, involving the SNS and adrenal cortex, which helps the body prepare for fight or flight. (pages 30, 31, 38)

**Synaptic gap/synapse** A small gap separating neurons. It consists of the presynaptic membrane (which discharges neurotransmitters), the postsynaptic membrane (containing receptor sites for neurotransmitters) and a synaptic gap between the two. The synaptic gap between a transmitting and receiving neuron is about 10 nm wide. (page 38)

**Systematic desensitisation** Based on classical conditioning (the behavioural approach), a therapy used to treat phobias and problems involving anxiety. A client is gradually exposed to the threatening situation under relaxed conditions until the anxiety reaction is extinguished. (pages 37, 56)

**Systematic sample** A method of obtaining a representative sample by selecting every, for example, 5th or 10th person. (page 25)

**Target population** The group of people that the researcher is interested in. The group of people from whom a sample is drawn and about whom generalisations can be made. (page 25)

**Temperament hypothesis** The view that attachment type can be explained in terms of an infant's innate temperament rather than caregiver sensitivity. (page 12)

**Terrorism** Any act intended to cause death or serious bodily harm to civilians with the purpose of intimidating a population or compelling a government to do, or abstain from, any act. (page 47)

**Test-retest reliability** A method used to check external reliability. The same test or interview is given to the same participants on two occasions to see if the same results are obtained. (pages 23, 32)

**Time sampling** An observational technique in which the observer records behaviours in a given time frame, e.g. noting what a target individual is doing every 30 seconds. (page 22)

**Type A personality** A tendency to approach life in a certain way, characterised by, for example, competitiveness and impatience. It is believed to increase the risk of coronary heart disease. (page 35)

**UCR** *see* unconditioned response.

**UCS** *see* unconditioned stimulus.

**Unconditioned response (UCR)** In classical conditioning, the innate reflex response to a stimulus, such as salivating when presented with food. (page 11)

**Unconditioned stimulus (UCS)** In classical conditioning, the stimulus that inevitably produces an innate reflex response, such as food producing a salivation response. (page 11)

**Unstructured interview** An interview that starts out with some general aims and possibly some questions, and lets the interviewee's answers guide subsequent questions. (pages 20, 22)

**Unstructured observation** An observer records all relevant behaviour but has no system. This technique may be chosen because the behaviour to be studied is largely unpredictable. (page 22)

**Validity** The extent to which a study and its findings are legitimate or true. (pages 6, 8, 13, 14, 15, 22, 23, 28, 31, 32, 35, 40, 41, 43, 55)

**Vicarious reinforcement** Learning which is not through direct reinforcement of behaviour, but through observing someone else being reinforced for that behaviour. (page 52)

**Visual cache** In the working memory model, a component of the visuo-spatial sketchpad which deals with the storage of visual information, such as the arrangement of objects. (page 5)

**Visuo-spatial sketchpad** In the working memory model, a component which encodes visual information. Divided into the visual cache (stores information) and inner scribe (spatial relations). (page 5)

**Volunteer bias** A form of sampling bias. Occurs because volunteer participants are usually more highly motivated than randomly selected participants. (page 25)

**Volunteer sample** A sample of participants produced by asking for volunteers. Sometimes referred to as a 'self-selected' sample. (page 25)

**Weapon focus effect** In violent crimes, an eyewitness' attention may be drawn to the weapon held by a criminal, reducing their ability to remember other details, such as the criminal's face. (page 7)

**Withdrawal symptoms** Abnormal physical or psychological reactions to the abrupt discontinuation of a drug to which an individual has developed physical dependence. (page 38)

**Word-length effect** People remember lists of short words better than lists of long words, governed by the capacity of the phonological loop. (page 5)

**Working memory model (WMM)** An explanation of short-term memory, called 'working memory'. Based on four components, some with storage capacity. (page 5)

**Workload** The demands of a person's work role. This can be stressful because it is repetitive, high intensity, monotonous or high volume. (page 34)

**Workplace stressors** Aspects of our working environment that we experience as stressful, and which cause a stress reaction in our body. (page 34)

**Yerkes-Dodson law** The curvilinear relationship between arousal and performance – people do not perform well when they are very relaxed, they perform best when moderately aroused and performance drops again at high levels of arousal. (page 7)

**Zero correlation** Co-variables are not linked. (page 26)